In Him

A Study of Ephesians

Katie M. Peters

© 2022 Kathleen M. Peters
All rights reserved. No part of this book may be reproduced or used in any manner without written permission of the copyright owner except for use of quotations in a book review.

This work includes illustrative stories which are works of fiction in which names, characters, places, and incidents are either the product of the author's imagination or used fictitiously. Any resemblance to actual persons, living or dead, events, or locals is entirely coincidental.

First paperback edition Dec 2022
Ebook editions and second paperback edition Dec 2024

Unless indicated otherwise, scripture quotations are taken from the (NASB®) New American Standard Bible®, Copyright © 1960, 1971, 1977, 1995, 2020 by The Lockman Foundation.
Used by permission. All rights reserved. www.lockman.org

ISBN 979-8-9880538-0-4 (paperback)
ISBN 979-8-9880538-1-1 (pdf)
ISBN 979-8-9880538-2-8 (ePub)
ISBN 979-8-9880538-3-5 (kindle)

Cover design by Katie M. Peters

Published by Hope Is Calling
www.HopeIsCalling.com

Introduction

~*~ Ephesians 1:1 Paul, an apostle of Christ Jesus by the will of God, To the saints who are at Ephesus and are faithful in Christ Jesus: 2 Grace to you and peace from God our Father and the Lord Jesus Christ.

Thus begins Paul's letter to the Ephesian church.

Ephesus was a city in ancient Turkey, so this is a church that primarily consisted of Gentiles who had come to believe in Jesus Christ.

To me, Ephesians is one of the greatest and most overlooked books in the New Testament. It is full of truths that are life-transforming when illuminated by the Holy Spirit.

So welcome to this Bible Study! You will find many scriptures throughout this study. We will go through every single verse in Ephesians, and all of them will be like two verses above, larger print, bold, and with ~*~ leading.

You'll also find many other scriptures that tie together with Ephesians and which help us to understand what Paul is referencing. Those will be set off with ~~~~~~, so it's easy for you to identify what is scripture and what is just me sharing my thoughts.

It's okay if you disagree with what I share that is not scripture! Talk with God about everything, and He will "open the eyes of your heart" to see what He wants *you* to discover! (We will talk about that phrase later on in chapter one.)

There are writing prompts throughout this book, since I and many others find that jotting down thoughts while we spend time with God helps to tune our ears to hear Him and receive revelation. If you're reading an ebook version, then may I recommend a journal that you can write it as you go? If this is the paperback version of this book, then you can write in the book directly!

Before we dive into this letter, I would like to go over a few fundamentals that I believe are pivotal for understanding this amazing book of the Bible.

Supernatural God

We have to start with the acknowledgement that God is a supernatural God! He does things that are outside our comprehension, and the only way to understand is by His Spirit.

John recorded that Jesus said *this* when He was trying to prepare His disciples for His imminent departure:

"These things I have spoken to you while remaining with you. 26 But the Helper, the Holy Spirit whom the Father will send in My name, He will teach you all things, and remind you of all that I said to you." (John 14:25)

Jesus was telling them that they still had a lot to learn. But learning everything was not something they had to tackle on their own, thank goodness! We could never figure out all the truths of God on our own! It is one of the functions of the Holy Spirit to teach us. Praise the Lord!

I will sometimes encourage you to write out thanksgiving or prayers or questions as you go through this study. This act of writing out what we're thinking and wondering is often a way of tuning our spiritual ears to hear what God wants to show us.

Make this study a conversation between you and the Holy Spirit of God. Write down what He shows you, for this will help you to "hold onto it!"

Let's pray: "Holy Spirit, thank You so much that You have indeed come to teach me all things. I know there are more things than my mind can comprehend, but You not only are able to open my mind to understand Your truths, but You also know when I am ready to learn each lesson, and You are able to teach me! You are able! Thank You for this! I therefore ask You to teach me Your truth. I ask in Jesus' Name, amen."

Depths

Ephesians is also very "deep." Often, Paul uses just a few words to reference a truth that is so deep and so profound and so life-changing (when illuminated by the Holy Spirit) that entire books have been written on that one truth alone!

So as we go through Ephesians, you might often find yourself with the feeling that you're still "missing something" or "you don't quite get it." That's okay. **You can still accept that truth and invite the reality of it into your life, even without understanding it.**

~~~~~~~~~
Proverbs 3:5
Trust in the Lord with all your heart
And do not lean on your own understanding.
~~~~~~~~~

This is one of the most famous verses in the Bible, but I think sometimes we quote it without actually thinking about what it means.

What actually is meant by "your own understanding"?

I believe it's not only the things we think we understand, but *it's also the judgements we make about the things we <u>don't</u> understand*. This is pivotal, for we tend to not believe the things we don't understand.

It is natural for us to evaluate everything we hear against the evidence of our experience. If we do not see the evidence of it, then we reject it as false. The problem is that this rejection is leaning on our own understanding.

The big problem with this is that *everything* that we receive from God must be received by faith, and faith is a proof of things *not* seen/understood.

~~~~~~~~~~
Hebrews 11:1
Now faith is the certainty of things hoped for, a proof of things not seen.
~~~~~~~~~~

Also note that this verse above from Proverbs says to trust in the Lord with your **heart**. It does *not* say to trust in the Lord with your mind.

Sometimes we require more to believe God than we do a perfect stranger. We can meet a rocket scientist, and we'll believe anything he says about rockets. We know this guy who is an incredible car mechanic, and we believe whatever he says about what our car needs. But when the God who created this world and our life tells us something about it, we sometimes struggle to believe Him!

We must *expect* that there will be many times when we are presented with something in the Word of God which appears exactly opposite of what we have seen so far in our lives—things that we cannot understand with our mind.

This is when we are faced with the choice described in Proverbs 3:5. We can *either* lean (or rely) on what our own mind understands of what we have seen and experienced, *or* we can trust in what our Lord is saying.

What does this look like in practice?

When I am reading something in the Bible that makes me feel that way, this is how I pray: "Father, thank You for giving me Your Word. You could have left us to be ignorant and lost in sin and depression and darkness, yet You sent Jesus to save us. You sent Your Word to tell us about it! I do not understand this part that I just read. But I am choosing to believe that this Word is true because You said it. Holy Spirit, Jesus said that You were sent to teach us all things, so my request is that You would teach me this, in the time and method of Your choosing. Thank You for Your love for me. Amen."

Circles and tapestry

Paul talks in circles, not in a line.

In American culture, "talking in circles" is usually considered to be derogatory, because we like things to move in a straight line, be explained in an orderly fashion, and happen in an order that makes sense. To us, time (and everything in it) moves in a line, on a timeline.

But God doesn't live in a timeline. The truths of God overlap each other and weave together in a beautiful tapestry circling back around to build higher and higher and higher to transform lives in ways that are impossible in a natural timeline. Paul's writing reflects this.

As we move through Ephesians, you'll notice that instead of a straight line, Paul's focus is sometimes more like this:

Understanding this helps us not to feel lost when Paul circles around from one topic to another and back again.

In Christ

The phrase "in Christ/in Him" is a key phrase in Ephesians! I encourage you to highlight each instance in your Bible or write them down as you see them, for they are pivotal. I will underline them as I did above, in the first verse.

What does "in Him" mean?
Consider this bit of biology.
A female is born with all the eggs she will ever have in her ovaries. So think of your maternal biological grandmother—the mother of your mother.

Once upon a time, one of her eggs was fertilized. It went on to divide and multiply and became your mother. This means that **before your mother was born, the egg that eventually became half of you was already there**, microscopically small inside her ovaries—which were inside your grandmother's womb.

You were "in" not only your mother when she was pregnant with you, but that one egg—half of what eventually became you—was in your grandmother as well!

This is the closest natural comparison I can think of to represent what God means when He says we are "in Christ," so it is a metaphor that I will refer back to later in this study.

Now consider adoption.
In the natural, adoption changes only the legal parental rights and responsibilities for a child. It transfers those legal rights from the natural parents to the adoptive parents. But humans cannot change DNA. An adopted child still retains a part of the nature of their genetic parents.

But if we *could* change DNA, *then* this would be like what God does spiritually when we become His children. Spiritually, we are His children, and we are therefore "in Christ Jesus." Not only are we His according to spiritual laws, He also places us "in Christ Jesus" in a way that changes our very nature.

How is this possible? Well, it *wouldn't* be possible if He weren't a supernatural God! Look for the evidence of this as we read through the rest of chapter one!

Writing Prompt

But first, what do you hope to receive and gain through this study? Write your desires, but ask God what *His* desires for you are as well. Start a conversation with God!

_____
_____
_____
_____
_____
_____
_____
_____
_____
_____
_____
_____
_____
_____
_____
_____
_____

Chapter One

Let's go through the rest of chapter one! It's all about the spiritual position, status, and state of being that exist, both for Jesus and for us. This is foundational, as we'll discover!

Remember to notice every place where Paul talks about us being <u>in Christ</u>! I'll continue underlining them.

~*~ Eph 1:3 Blessed be the God and Father of our Lord Jesus Christ, who has blessed us with every spiritual blessing in the heavenly places <u>in Christ,</u>

Let's look at this verse more closely and start by asking some questions.

How many spiritual blessings does this verse say God has blessed us with? Only some of them or all of them?

Think about the reality of that, and ask yourself first if you really believe that God has blessed you with *every* spiritual blessing. You may find yourself considering areas of lack in your life and wondering how it's possible for you to *really* be so blessed if this or that is happening (or not happening) in your life. If you're like me, then you might already be facing your first choice of whether or not to lean on your own understanding!

The next question is this: what kind of blessing is Paul talking about?

He said nothing about financial blessings (though 3 John 1:2 mentions those), and he said nothing about favor with man (though Proverbs 3:4 does.) He's talking specifically about *spiritual* blessings, and that is what this book is full of!

The final question is this: do we receive these blessings by ourselves, standing on our own?

No! Our receipt of these blessings is *entirely* dependent upon the fact that we are in Christ!

Writing Prompts

What do you think spiritual blessings actually are?
What spiritual blessings do you see already in your life?
What are some spiritual blessings that you don't see in your life *yet*?

My prayer is that as you study Ephesians, God will increase the spiritual blessings in your life, for His glory and for the benefit of both you and the world around you!

_____

_____

_____

_____

_____

_____

~*~ Eph 1:4 just as He chose us <u>in Him</u> before the foundation of the world, that we would be holy and blameless before Him.

 This verse says that we are chosen, but there are those words "<u>in Him</u>" again. This is very important, but first let's look at *when* God chose us, for He did not choose us when we chose Him. Nor did He choose us when we were born. He didn't even choose us the moment we were conceived.

 According to this verse, **He chose us before the foundation of the world.** He is outside of time, and He has always known the entire timeline of human history that exists on this world He created. Back before the world's foundation was laid, *that* is when we were chosen.

 Note that this doesn't mean that our decision to choose Him never existed, for God already knew, before the foundation of the world, that we *would* choose Him. Salvation is therefore a mutual decision to between us and God to choose each other, just as a marriage is when a man and a woman both choose each other. (In fact, we'll see in chapter five that marriage is a symbol of Christ and the church!)

~~~~~~~~~
Ephesians 5:31
For this reason a man shall leave his father and his mother and be joined to his wife, and the two shall become one flesh. 32 This mystery is great; but I am speaking with reference to Christ and the church.
~~~~~~~~

 Now we can see how it is possible for us to have been chosen in Him before the foundations of the world! It had already been decided that Jesus would be crucified for the sins of the world and rise victorious. God knew that we would believe and choose Him, and He decided that the method through which He would give us a new nature was by placing us in Christ Jesus, so that He would be the head and we would be the body.

~~~~~~~~~

John 17:20

"I am not asking on behalf of these alone, but also for those who believe in Me through their word, 21 that they may all be one; just as You, Father, are in Me and I in You, that they also may be in Us, so that the world may believe that You sent Me."

~~~~~~~~~

The next part of Ephesians 1:4 answers the question of what His intention was in choosing us in this way. The answer is this: that we would be holy and blameless.

But what does *that* mean?

The word "holy" means "set apart" or "separate." When we say God is holy, we are saying He is separate from anything and anyone else. He is not like anything or anyone else.

So when the Bible uses the word "holy" to describe things or people, it is saying the thing or person is set apart for God. BLB Thayer's Lexicon says it means "prepared for God."

Blameless means without blemish. It means you cannot be blamed.

Together, these reflect a chosen sacrifice. The command by God in the old sacrificial system was for lambs to be carefully selected. They would find those without blemish and set them apart from the rest until the sacrifice.

The Bible teaches that Jesus took our sin. This is the only way that we can be blameless in the sight of God who knows every thought and every deed we have ever done or ever will do.

But, because God sees us "in Christ Jesus," He *does* see us as blameless! He is not ignorant of the sins we have committed, but He has decreed that we can no longer be blamed for them because Jesus took that blame upon Himself.

Let's consider an illustration.
Pretend that there's a woman whose job involves quality control in a factory. She's responsible for making sure a certain machine is set up properly so that the products are cut to the right specifications.
The machine's alignment gets off, and for some reason she misses it. A whole days' worth of products are cut wrong… and those products *had* to be completed that day to fill an extremely important order.
She knows that because of her mistake, the order won't get filled. The customer will probably cancel the contract because that's how big of a deal it is for the order to get filled on time. The company will blame her because it was her mistake.
But then suddenly, at the end of the day, this guy who runs another line says, "No worries. My machine was set up correctly and I had it making those exact products all day long. My products will fill the order. You will not be blamed. I can actually use the products that your line made over here for another order."
Did the women still make the mistake? Yes, she did! And in a human world, she would possibly be fired anyway.
But they cannot blame her for the order not being filled, because it *was* filled! They cannot even blame her for wasting material, because the product was used to fill a different order!

This is an example of how *we* can be called "blameless." We make mistakes, but we are still blameless <u>in Him</u>. We cannot be blamed because of what Jesus did on our behalf. He measures up to the standard because He was truly blameless. And *what He has done counts for us*. He takes our mess and offers us His perfection in return!

Notice however, that being blameless in Him includes being holy/set apart/dedicated to God.

We have a say in whether we will become "set apart" for Him.

It does not say that we would live our lives for ourselves and still be blameless. We must realize that we have been set apart to live a life set apart.

So what does it mean to be set apart or dedicated to God (holy)?

Does it mean that we have to be a pastor or preacher or have some other ministry position? No! But what it *does* mean is something that will be unique and special to each one of us.

Writing Prompts

What has God called you to do? It may include motherhood or sisterhood, being a wife, being a saleswomen, working a factory job, grocery shopping for a family, being a businesswoman, teaching, etc.

List the 3-5 main areas and responsibilities in your life. One might be your job, or another might be your relationship(s) with particular people. Perhaps you volunteer somewhere or are regularly involved in a hobby or pastime.

_____

_____

_____

_____

_____

_____

_____

_____

_____
_____
_____
_____
_____
_____
_____
_____

    Now ask God to show you what it looks like to dedicate that part of your life to God.

    I want to challenge you *not* to think of measurable standards. This is not an exercise in listing out high human standards that we probably will never measure up to.

    I'll use grocery shopping as an example. What does dedicating our grocery shopping to God look like? Our mind might immediately jump to things like "buying healthy foods" or "staying within a budget." Those are good things, but many people whose lives are not dedicated to God have those same good goals!

    Perhaps dedicating our grocery shopping to God means listening for His whisper to direct us if a shopper beside us needs someone to pray for them. Perhaps dedicating our grocery shopping to God might sometimes mean breaking the budget and trusting Him if He says, "Buy extra food and invite the family next door over for a cookout this weekend." Perhaps it means willingness to pay for the groceries of the person behind us in line when He gives that prompt… regardless of whether they look like a drug addict or a successful businessman! (Because if we're honest, we're likely to think the successful businessman doesn't need it and the drug addict wouldn't need it if they'd spend their money on food instead of drugs. But God knows if the successful-looking businessman might have just lost his wife, house and much of what he owns in a divorce. He also knows if the drug addict prayed just that morning that God would give her a sign if He really exists and loves her!)

Writing Prompt

So quiet your mind for a few minutes and ask God to show you what He thinks dedicating each of the parts of *your* life to Him might look like. Write down the thoughts and questions that come to you as you talk to Him about it.

_____

_____

_____

_____

_____

_____

_____

_____

_____

_____

_____

_____

_____

_____

So...are *you* set apart to God and blameless? Yes or No?

If "no" is the answer that came to mind, then consider this: are you looking at yourself in the here and now, considering what you see in your life? Or do you believe that *God,* looking at you from a perspective that is outside of time, *sees you* as set apart and blameless? This is not a question of what you see. It's a question of whether you believe what God says *He* sees. Can you believe that He knows what He's going to work in your life in the days and months and years ahead?

Do you struggle with this? Most of us do! But here again we have the choice between our own understanding and His.

Here in Ephesians, it says that God *did* choose us that we would be set apart and blameless. His Word is telling us what He sees as reality.

Let's choose to say, "Lord, Your word says You have chosen me to be set apart and blameless. I struggle to understand that, but I am choosing here and now to trust what You say more than my own understanding. You know how much I don't understand, but I believe that You know what You're talking about. Holy Spirit, be my teacher and show me what I need to understand. I ask this in Jesus' Name, because I am in Him."

The next verse tells us more about *how* we are in Jesus.

~*~ Eph 1:5 (In love) He predestined us to adoption as sons and daughters through Jesus Christ to Himself, according to the good pleasure of His will, 6 to the praise of the glory of His grace, with which He favored us in the Beloved.

Jesus is the only begotten Son of God. So therefore, if we are "in Him," then this is how we are also God's sons and daughters. Galatians talks more about how we are adopted:

~~~~~~~~~
Galatians 4:4

But when the fullness of the time came, God sent His Son, born of a woman, born under the Law, 5 so that He might redeem those who were under the Law, that we might receive the adoption as sons and daughters. 6 Because you are sons, God has sent the Spirit of His Son into our hearts, crying out, "Abba! Father!" 7 Therefore you are no longer a slave, but a son; and if a son, then an heir through God. Whom He foreknew, he predestined to become conformed to the image of His Son so that He would have many sons and daughters.
~~~~~~~~~

After Paul references our adoption, he continues with three amazing statements in this verse:

1. "According to the good pleasure of His will"

The words "according to" indicate a standard. Rockets are fired into space *according to* a carefully planned schedule and directions or it won't launch the satellite where it needs to be. In order for furniture to be assembled correctly, it must be put together *according to* the directions or it won't come out right.

In the same way, God has chosen us to be sons and daughters *according to* what He decided He wants to do, because He finds pleasure in doing it!

2. "To the praise of the glory of His grace"

He did this to show His power and His grace! Yes, He loves us, but all of this is meant to bring glory to Him as well!

Think of a time in history or a story where someone wealthy found pleasure in giving large gifts to people. The person may have genuinely given the things because they found pleasure in being able to do that for people. But the size of the gifts also is a natural testimony of his wealth, right?

So also, the amazing greatness of God's choice to adopt so many is a natural testimony of the greatness of His grace!

3. "With which He favored us in the Beloved."

And after all of that, Paul takes it one step farther. He says, "Okay. This amazing, glorious, powerful grace that does this? Not only does God have it, but He bestows it upon us!" He favors us with it! Wow.

~*~ Eph 1:7 <u>In Him</u> we have redemption through His blood, the forgiveness of our wrongdoings, according to the riches of His grace 8 which He lavished on us.

The redemption of our sins is not something He did and handed out to us. It is something He did which we can partake of if we are <u>in Him</u>.

Again, Paul underscores that this forgiveness is according to the riches of His grace, not our own efforts. Not because we did penance. Not because we proved we're good enough.

I love that it's the *riches* of His grace and not the poverty of His grace! The word "riches" speaks of abundance. It means more grace than is needed, no matter how great the sin or how high the price of redemption is!

Going back to redemption—if you have something of value and you get into such a bad situation that you sell that item to a pawn shop for money, the price to redeem it is set quite high. If you park in the wrong spot and your car is towed away, you have to pay to redeem it.

In the same way, it costs something to redeem us. The cost was Jesus's blood, of course, but let's think about it a little deeper. Would a person redeem their car from the impound lot or redeem their jewelry from the pawn shop only to park it in the wrong spot again or pawn it again? No! **For the redemption to be permanent, it has to be part of a much bigger plan—a much bigger change of situation.**

So too, God's redemption of us is much bigger than just Jesus's one-time payment for our sin. Ephesians is all about explaining the *complete change of situation* that makes our redemption permanent!

It's according to the riches of His grace! His riches are so great that there does not exist any sin so great that His riches cannot pay the cost of full, complete, *permanent* redemption!

Writing Prompt

Is there anything in your life that you struggle to believe has been (or can be) redeemed? It might be something you've done, but it also might be faults or failures that you consider unredeemable. This isn't about whether you've seen His redemption already; this is about whether you're willing to choose to believe that He is capable of doing what He says right here in His word that He has done. I encourage you to write out a statement, here and now, that offers these things to God, confessing that you believe that Jesus' blood truly does have the power of full redemption in your life!

_____

_____

_____

_____

_____

_____

_____

_____

~*~ Eph 1: In all wisdom and insight 9 He made known to us the mystery of His will, according to His good pleasure which He [the Father] set forth in Him [Jesus], 10 regarding His plan of the fullness of the times, to bring all things together in Christ, things in the heavens and things on the earth.

    Again Paul repeats the phrase "according to His good pleasure." And again I love realizing how God finds pleasure in doing all these amazing things for us, His children and creation!
    But what is this mystery of His will? It is this adoption! This thing that doesn't make sense to our natural minds, and yet God says He did it anyway, simply because He decided to do it—He made it part of His will—because He found pleasure in doing it.

~~~~~~~~~~
Colossians 1:13

For He rescued us from the domain of darkness, and transferred us to the kingdom of His beloved Son, [Jesus] 14 in whom we have redemption, the forgiveness of sins. 15 He [Jesus] is the image of the invisible God, the firstborn of all creation: 16 ... all things have been created through Him and for Him... 19 For it was the Father's good pleasure for all the fullness to dwell in Him [Jesus], 20 and through Him [Jesus] to reconcile all things to Himself [the Father].

~~~~~~~~~~

God's goal is this: the new state of permanence that permits us to be redeemed completely. This is what Paul means by "His plan of the fullness of the times, to bring all things together in Christ."

This has always been the goal and the theme of the story. If the world's history was a movie, this would be that little blurb that the announcer uses to describe it: "God's plan to bring all things together in Christ to redeem the world and reconcile us to Himself."

Then the end of the verse clarifies which kinds of things: "Things in the heavens and things on the earth." This echoes what Jesus prayed when He said, "Your will be done on earth as it is in Heaven."

It is worthwhile to think about *how* God's will can be done on earth as it is in Heaven. It is tempting to sometimes just think that we don't play a part in it other than to just pray that His will be done. And yet, when God created people, He said that He had given *us* the dominion over the earth.

Romans chapter twelve, 2 Corinthians chapter twelve, and later verses and chapters of Ephesians all talk about how we are the body of Christ. We are His hands and feet!

So God's *method* of achieving His will here on earth is through us! Jesus is the head, giving directions, and we are the body, doing the actions. His will is done here on earth "as it is in heaven" when we obey Him explicitly, in everything, the same way a functioning hand or foot obeys the instructions that our brain sends.

We'll talk about this more in chapter three and chapter four.

~*~ Eph 1:11 <u>In Him</u> we also have obtained an inheritance, having been predestined according to the purpose of Him who works all things in accordance with the plan of His will, 12 to the end that we who were the first to hope <u>in Christ</u> would be to the praise of His glory.

We have "obtained an inheritance." This means that not only are we sons and daughters of a Father God who has abundant spiritual riches, we are *heirs*!

Also notice that the words "have obtained" are past tense. This means that God has already given it to us. It's ours, even if we don't understand the full extent of it.

I want to repeat that. *Even if you don't understand what you have inherited, that doesn't mean that you aren't an heir.* Consider little Prince George of England. He's in line to the throne of England. That is his inheritance, even though he probably doesn't have the slightest idea what it means right now. He will probably understand by the time his father becomes king, but he is too young to understand now.

We are children of the King of Kings! Even when our spiritual maturity is too "young" to comprehend what it means, that doesn't invalidate our inheritance. It is ours, and it exists, and it is real! Maturity is needed for us to fully understand it.

Does this inheritance seem real to you, or do you struggle to comprehend it? I think it's safe to say that very few humans understand fully what this inheritance actually includes, for "the fullness of the times" that Paul mentioned in verse 10 has not yet come. And yet, if this is God's goal, then the closer we get to the end times, the closer we are also getting to this "fullness" being realized!

Writing Prompt

Think about what this "fullness" might actually mean *for you!* I encourage you to write down either questions for God, a prayer reflecting your heart, or whatever response you find His Spirit echoing inside of you as you consider this fullness.

_____
_____
_____
_____
_____
_____
_____
_____
_____
_____
_____
_____
_____
_____
_____
_____
_____

Then the verse again goes on to say, "according to." So *again* Paul emphasizes that all of this is according to God's purposes and His will and His plans. The devil often tries to make us think that God won't do this or that because we have committed this sin or failed to do this or that good thing. But these are his lies, whispered to us in an attempt to make us think that God does things according to our actions. *He doesn't!* God does not make us heirs because we deserve it or even because we asked for it. He makes us heirs because He planned this, and it fits what He wants to accomplish in the world.

Our status as heirs does not invalidate the natural order of sowing and reaping (consequences) that exist on the earth. But we are talking about something much greater. We are talking about what God has chosen to do *according to His pleasure, His purpose, His plan, and His will.*

Which do we think really has greater weight? The actions of little us? Or the will and purpose of God?

Does it matter what we do? Yes! We can fight this great and powerful purpose and will of God (which would kind of be like fighting a tsunami—pointless and destined to beat you up and make you feel like everything you try to do gets you nowhere)—or we can dive in, immerse ourselves in this amazing will of God, and be carried along by His power!

Do we want our will, or His will?
_ I want my will.
_ I want His will.

Now that we know what His will is, why would we ever want our own will?

~*~ Eph 1:13 In Him, you also, after listening to the message of truth, the gospel of your salvation— having also believed, you were sealed in Him with the Holy Spirit of the promise, 14 who is a first installment of our inheritance, in regard to the redemption of God's own possession, to the praise of His glory.

Look how often Paul emphasizes how we are in Him! We aren't just kind of in Him or sometimes there, we are *sealed* in Him!

~~~~~~~~~~
John 14:20
"You will know that I am in My Father, and you are in Me, and I in you."
~~~~~~~~~~
John 17:20
"I am not asking on behalf of these alone, but also for those who believe in Me through their word, 21 that they may all be one; just as You, Father, are in Me and I in You, that they also may be in Us, so that the world may believe that You sent Me."
~~~~~~~~~~

How are we sealed? With the Holy Spirit… who is now in us!

The Holy Spirit in Hebrew is Ruach ha-kodesh, which means "the breath of God." He is our spiritual breath, giving us life. Without Him, we cannot spiritually live! So if we are truly spiritually alive, it is important that we understand it is because of His Spirit—His breath! It's not because of anything we're doing.

This Holy Breath is the first installment of our inheritance! Everything else follows from His indwelling.

Our permanent redemption starts *here*—His Breath giving us spiritual life. If we breath His Breath, then we are His possession! We are not our own.

Think of a heart transplant recipient. Their entire physical body is alive because of someone else's heart beating in their chest.

So it is with us. Our spiritual self is alive because of Someone Else's breath giving us life. *Every single breath we take.* We cannot get away from it, because without His Breath we cannot live spiritually!

So it is that we are in Him. And His very Breath and Spirit are now in us. This is God's intention for how we are to experience this redemption.

Writing Prompt

What does His Spirit being your very breath mean to you? Ask Him to show you something new about this reality! Write out your questions and thoughts to Him and write down anything He shows you!

_____
_____
_____
_____
_____
_____
_____
_____
_____
_____
_____
_____

~*~ Eph 1:15 For this reason I too, having heard of the faith <u>in the Lord Jesus</u> which exists among you and your love for all the saints, 16 do not cease giving thanks for you, while making mention of you in my prayers;

 Paul is setting us up for his first great prayer for the Ephesian church, and he models Jesus's example by starting his prayer with thanksgiving.
 In this great prayer, the list of things that Paul prays for them is a rundown of spiritual revelations that transform lives. These verses are my very favorite in the entire Bible, and I pray that *you* will also come to understand them and love them as much as I do!

~*~ **Eph 1:17** (I pray) that the God of our Lord Jesus Christ, the Father of glory, may give you a spirit of wisdom and of revelation in the knowledge of Him.

    The first thing that Paul prays for them is the **spirit of wisdom.** Wisdom is more than knowledge. Wisdom is knowing how to apply knowledge and understanding the proper context of that knowledge. When you understand the technicalities of how to drive a car and change lanes, you have knowledge. When you are able to determine when it is and isn't wise to change lanes on an eight-lane highway, you have wisdom.

    The second thing that Paul prays for them is **revelation in the knowledge of Him.** Revelation is the only way to truly know Him. Jesus's conversation with Peter gives us a clearer idea of the specific revelation that Paul is talking about here:

~~~~~~~~~

Matthew 16:16

Simon Peter answered, "You are the Christ, the Son of the living God." 17 And Jesus said to him, "Blessed are you, Simon Barjona, because flesh and blood did not reveal this to you, but My Father who is in heaven. 18 And I also say to you that you are Peter, and upon this rock I will build My church; and the gates of Hades will not overpower it.

~~~~~~~~~

    Jesus was pointing out that Peter's confession was more than just head knowledge. Jesus knew that Peter wasn't just stating empty words. He was making a confession of a truth that he believed—a truth that had already started completely changing the course of his life.

    Jesus further stated that this knowledge of who He really was *can only be understood by revelation*. This means that although it is knowledge, it comes to our spirit. It's not something that can be understood as the result of effort by the brain.

Compare a child who has an absent father—who knows the name of their father but has never known them—with a child who has been held by their father every day, who has been cared for by their father when they're sick, who knows the things that make their father smile and laugh, and who runs to see their father when he comes home every day.
Both can identify, "You are my father." Only one has the full revelation of what it means to have a father.

Many people can say that Jesus was the Christ: the anointed One and Son of God. But there are people who know it in their head only, and then there are people who have the full revelation. Like Peter, it changes their lives.
This—this revelation of who Jesus is that changes lives—*this* is the foundation that Jesus said His church was going to be built on.

All of this is why Paul prayed that the people of Ephesus would receive **the revelation** of the knowledge of Jesus. The church could not grow without it then, and it cannot grow without it today either! At least, *real* growth cannot happen without this revelation.

~*~ Eph 1:18 I pray that the eyes of your heart may be enlightened,

Here is the next thing on Paul's list of what he prays for them— that **the eyes of their heart may be enlightened!** He is talking about enlightenment because of the spiritual darkness that exists because of sin. Only the light of God can pierce through it!

Many verses in the Bible reference this.
When Paul was on trial, he recounted to King Agrippa how Jesus said this when He appeared to him on the road to Damascus:

~~~~~~~~~~
Acts 26:12

"For this purpose I have appeared to you, to appoint you as a servant and a witness…to the Gentiles, to whom I am sending you, 18 to open their eyes so that they may turn from darkness to light, and from the power of Satan to God, that they may receive forgiveness of sins and an inheritance among those who have been sanctified by faith in Me."
~~~~~~~~~~

David said this:

~~~~~~~~~~
2 Samuel 22:29

"For You are my lamp, Lord;
And the Lord illuminates my darkness."
~~~~~~~~~~

And here are more references:

~~~~~~~~~~
Job 12:22

He reveals mysteries from the darkness,
And brings the deep darkness into light.
~~~~~~~~~~
Matthew 6:23

"But if your eye is bad, your whole body will be full of darkness. So if the light that is in you is darkness, how great is the darkness!
~~~~~~~~~~

Verses 18 and 19 continues Paul's prayer, and here he shifts to three things he wants them to know. I'm going to break them out, one-by-one.

~*~ Eph 1:18 (continued)...so that you will know the hope of His calling,

This is the first thing that Paul prays that they will know: **the hope of His calling.**

The words "so that" indicate that having the eyes of your heart enlightened is the way to the hope of His calling. But what actually is the hope of His calling? Consider these verses from Romans:

~~~~~~~~~~

Romans 8:28

We know that God causes all things to work together for good to those who love God, to those who are called according to His purpose. 29 For those whom He foreknew, He also predestined to become conformed to the image of His Son, so that He would be the firstborn among many brothers and sisters; 30 and these whom He predestined, He also called; and these whom He called, He also justified; and these whom He justified, He also glorified.

~~~~~~~~~~

Verse 28 of this passage in Romans ends with "to those who are *called* according to His purpose," so verse 29 goes on to declare what God's purpose actually is. It's saying, "This is His goal for the end of the story. This is why He uses everything for good in your life... because He is not content for Jesus to be His only child. He's not content to have Jesus be the only one who walked like Jesus walked. His purpose is for there to be many brothers and sisters who also walk like Jesus did!"

Verses 29 and 30 sum up the story. *Our story.* Take a look at this four-part story:
1. Those whom He foreknew, He also **predestined**...
2. and these whom He predestined, He also **called**;
3. and these whom He called, He also **justified**;
4. and these whom He justified, He also **glorified**.

First, He **predestined** us. Since God exists outside of time, He knew the entire story of our lives before time even began. We cannot get away from what He knows will happen—not because we don't have free will to make choices, but because He already knows what our choices will be. He knows what choices other people will make that affect us and the next choices we'll make in response, and so forth. He doesn't waste that knowledge! He has planned—predestined—things that He will show us and do for us at thousands of pivotal moments along the way so that He can bring us to that end goal that He desires.

That is where this verse's story begins, with that predestination outside of time. That is part one.

The second part of the story is when He **calls** us.

This is when He steps inside the Timeline of our story, and we hear His call to follow Him.

The gospels recount the stories of when Jesus called a number of the disciples, and the Bible also recounts the moment when Saul was called, when Isaiah and Jeremiah were called, when Moses was called, and many others.

Each of us also had a moment in our lives when we first heard His call. Many times, it took us a while to identify what that call actually was and then make the decision to answer it, but the call was there, inside of our life's timeline!

When we answer the call, He **justifies** us.

That means that He takes the sacrifice that Jesus made on the cross, and God applies it to our account.

If we compare it to an accountant who is doing the books for a company, they're looking at this big balance that is on the books for me, that I owe. But then there's also this absolutely perfect payment that Jesus made.

When I answered God's call, He said, "Okay, that payment is now credited to your account," and when that credit was written down, the balance of my debt became zero. It was *justified*. Perfectly balanced.

The final part of the story is that He **glorifies** us.

This is perhaps the hardest part to comprehend because God—telling the story from His viewpoint outside of time—is telling it in past tense. He says that I am glorified!

This is a continuation of His choice to justify me. For just as He has credited Jesus's death on the cross to my account to pay my debt, so also He has credited the glory of Jesus's triumph over death when He rose again to my account!

I'm stuck inside this Timeline of my life where it's hard to see it, but if I believe He cannot lie and His words are true, then this is true as well! I am glorified!

What does this have to do with the hope of His calling?

Here is the answer:

In that four-part timeline, there is only one part that we humans can easily grab a hold of.

The call.

The **predestination** happens before time began. We weren't there, and we weren't aware of it when it happened.

The **justification** is something that we cannot possibly understand unless He gives us the revelation to understand it. There are probably right now hundreds of thousands of Christians who have heard and answered the call, but they still don't understand that they are justified.

The **glorification** is the end of the story—where He's taking us. In the many moments when we're looking for hope, that glorious end of the story doesn't feel real to us...which is why we're looking for hope.

But the calling—that's the part we know. That is the point in the four-part story that is placed into our hands.

The hope of His calling is this: the knowledge and revelation that the call that we hear is part of this four-part process and story.
It's not a call that stands on its own.
If you hear Him calling you, then you can rest assured that He **predestined** you before time began, otherwise you'd never hear Him calling you! Romans 8:30 assures you that the calling *is* a result of His predestination!
And then, if you answer the call, you can know what part three and part four are also! He **justifies** you, and He **glorifies** you! It doesn't really matter that our natural mind has a hard time wrapping itself around how we could be so full of glory that we become glorified. This verse assures us that if indeed we have heard the call, then being justified and glorified *is* where the story is going! He is doing it, and what He has started, He will finish!

~~~~~~~~~
Philippians 1:6
For I am confident of this very thing, that He who began a good work among you will complete it by the day of Christ Jesus.
~~~~~~~~~

This is the hope of His calling.
The hope is found in the knowledge that this calling that we hear *means so much more.*
The hope is found in the assurance that while we hear the call and answer the call by giving our lives to Him, *He does everything*

else. Notice that the verse doesn't say, "Those whom He calls must figure out how to justify themselves and work hard enough that eventually they'll become glorious because of how perfect they've become." Nope. Those whom He called, *He* justified, and those whom He justified, *He* glorified. *He does it*. All of Romans chapter eight reiterates this over and over again.

~~~~~~~~~~
Romans 8:31
What then shall we say to these things?
If God is for us, who is against us?
~~~~~~~~~~

Perhaps the most perfect reminder in all of it is how verse 31 ends this section of Romans. If God is for us, who can be against us? *Even our own self no longer counts against us.*

All we have to do, for Him to do His amazing work, is answer the call and give ourselves to Him. All we have to do is repeatedly choose not to take our lives back. To stay fully surrendered. And He'll do the rest!

Writing Prompt

Does this give you hope? Write out your prayer to God, thanking Him for the revelations and hope that He has already given you, and then tell Him what you desire from Him right now. Prayers like this are very powerful! Make this prayer a *real* reflection of *your* heart, and resist the urge to make it sound pretty. God treasures the rawness of our heart when we take it to Him!

_____

_____

_____

_____

Let's return to this prayer in Ephesians!

~*~ Eph 1: (v.18 continued)…and what are the riches of the glory of His inheritance in the saints

Here is the second thing Paul wants them to know: **the riches of the glory of His inheritance in the saints.** This phrase needs to be understood starting from the end and going back to the beginning.

First, who are the saints?
Strong's Concordance says that this word in the Greek is rarely used outside of the Bible. But in the Bible, it's used to designate things or people who are *set apart for God*.
This means that the word "saints" (which is often used in the New Testament) cannot be used for people who call themselves Christians but live life their own way, according to their own desires. It applies to those who have dedicated their life to God.

Second, what do these saints receive?
An inheritance. A glorious one! This reflects back to verse 11.

Third, is this inheritance a little inheritance?
Nope! Paul is praying that they would receive the revelation of the *riches* of this inheritance!
He's not talking about money. God knows as well as we do that money is a medium of exchange. It's needed to do many things in His kingdom, and He often supplies our needs by supplying money (though sometimes He supplies our needs in other ways). So these riches might *sometimes* include money, but Paul specifies that his desire is for them to know the riches *of the glory of His inheritance*.
The revelation of this inheritance includes things like the ability to walk through difficult circumstances and stay completely free of discouragement and depression. The ability to deal with difficult coworkers and still be joyful. The ability to see what's going on in the world and still rest in a deep river of peace that flows within you.

These things come from the revelation that starts with a revelation of the knowledge of who *He* is. We cannot receive what He wants us to receive until we understand who He really is. Only then can we understand this inheritance!

~*~ Eph 1:19 and what is the boundless greatness of His power toward us who believe.

This is the third thing Paul prays that they would know: **the boundless greatness of His power toward us.** I love that Paul isn't just praying for them to know God's power. He's praying that they know the *greatness* of His power!

Also notice that Paul again specifies that it's toward us who believe. Our willingness to believe what God says is key.

His power is an external thing while the riches of the inheritance is an inward thing. The external always follows the internal. We cannot receive the revelation of His power *toward* us until we first receive the revelation of His inheritance ***in*** us.

So often, Christians pray and plead to see the power, but we need to first pray to receive what has to come first: the revelation of the knowledge of Him and the revelation of the riches of the glory of His inheritance in us.

~*~ Eph 1: (v. 19 continued)... These are in accordance with the working of the strength of His might 20 which He brought about in Christ, when He raised Him from the dead and seated Him at His right hand in the heavenly places, 21 far above all rule and authority and power and dominion, and every name that is named, not only in this age but also in the one to come. 22 And He put all things in subjection under His feet,

As we know, Paul often talks in loops, tying the thing that he's talking about back to Jesus as the whole reason that any of what he's saying is even possible.

That's what he's doing here. He's saying, "Just in case you forgot or missed the significance of all of the "in Him" statements that I've made so far, I'm going to come right out and say it.

All of this is because of Jesus.

All of this is because of the power of Jesus.

All of this is because Jesus was raised from the dead and now sits at the right hand of the Father.

All of this is because Jesus isn't just *barely* above every other authority that exists and just barely more powerful than everything else. He is *far above* every other authority, and His power is *far above* every other power. And not only all authorities and powers that exist now, but all that will ever exist!"

~*~ Eph 1: (v.22 continued)…and made Him head over all things to the church, 23 which is His body, the fullness of Him who fills all in all.

And then, after we're once again thinking about the incredible power and glory and authority of Jesus, Paul circles back around to *us*. He states that Jesus is the head of the church, and we are His body.

And then Paul makes this mind-boggling statement. We—His body—are the fullness of Him who fills all in all.

He—Jesus—fills us so completely that without us, His body is not complete. Isn't that absolutely amazing?

The full, complete revelation-truth of this is so mind-boggling that it's not possible for us really understand it with our minds. But this is the whole reason that Paul is praying for all of these revelations! He *knows* that there is no way for us to really understand how we can be part of the fullness of Jesus Christ in all

His glory and perfection unless God gives us these many revelations.

Writing Prompts

"Translate" verses 17-19 into a prayer for yourself, so that you are requesting these same revelations from God for yourself. Put your name in the prayer, use "I" and "me," and make it your own prayer!

_____

_____

_____

_____

_____

_____

_____

_____

_____

_____

_____

_____

Now that we have pulled apart each verse in this chapter, go back through the whole chapter and read it out loud to yourself. **Don't rush.**

What verse is now most meaningful to you and why?

Chapter Two

Chapter two signals a shift. Now that Paul has clearly stated the spiritual realities of what Jesus accomplished, the focus shifts a little bit to talk about how that spiritual change is reflected here on earth.

I want to give you a warning before we dive into this chapter.
The devil has been trying for *centuries* to condemn Christians when they read this chapter. We read what we were without Jesus, and then the devil points out areas of our lives where these seem to still exist. We feel condemnation, and we feel like we need to redouble our efforts to "do better" and "stop sinning."

~~~~~~~~~~
Romans 8:1
There is now no condemnation at all for those who are in Christ Jesus.
~~~~~~~~~~

This is not the path to freedom! Galatians says a lot about this, and this isn't a study of Galatians, but I want to point out that Paul talks about all of this *after* he spent all of chapter one making sure you know *who you are in Christ Jesus.* Why? **Because freedom from sin is the natural result of revelation from God's Spirit.**

Living free from sin is *not* the result of trying harder. The fruit of the Spirit is exactly that—the fruit *of the Spirit.* It's not the fruit of you. When we see sin in our life, we are seeing nothing more and nothing less than *the fruit of us.* (By that, I mean a fruit of our natural fleshly self.) Yes, it's sin, and yes it matters.

So what's the right path if we aren't supposed to "try harder"?

As this chapter talks about sin, and as you see areas of your life where sin seems evident, and the devil (called "the accuser" in Revelation chapter twelve) tries to hit you with condemnation, here's what I want you to do: Face that sin and picture yourself holding it in your hands. Then raise it up to God, and say, "Jesus, *thank You* that You died to pay for this sin *and* to set me free from it! I believe that You did, and I praise You and thank You for my salvation! It doesn't look like I'm free from it yet to *my* eyes. *But You say I'm free*, so I'm letting go of it and trusting You. I'm asking You, Father, to give me whatever revelations You know I need to walk in the freedom that Jesus died to purchase for me. Because I want to glorify You through my life."

That is how we overcome sin. This is what the voice in Heaven meant in Revelation 12 when it declared that they overcame their accuser by "the blood of the Lamb (Jesus) and the word of our testimony." This is us testifying of what Jesus has done for us!

~~~~~~~~~

Revelation 12:10
Now the salvation, and the power, and the kingdom of our God and the authority of His Christ have come, for **the accuser of our brothers and sisters has been thrown down**, the one who accuses them before our God day and night.11 And **they overcame him because of the blood of the Lamb and because of the word of their testimony**

Praying this way is righteousness! Romans and Galatians and Hebrews all talk about how we are not righteous because of what we do and don't do. God counts us as righteous *when we believe.* That's what it means when the Bible says over and over again that the righteous live by faith.

~~~~~~~~~~
Galatians 3:11
Now it is evident that no one is justified before God by the law, for "**The righteous shall live by faith.**"
~~~~~~~~~~

I encourage you to practice believing and confessing this in your own life as we go through this chapter!

~*~ Eph 2:1 And you were dead in your offenses and sins,

There are two truths that this tiny verse holds, and we must receive the revelation of both of them.
1. We must recognize our spiritual death. We cannot really live in a new life until we truly understand just how dead we are/were otherwise. I say "are" because not all people have accepted this new life, in which case the statement that they are dead still applies to them.
2. We must recognize the fact that—for us who believe—it is past tense.

I *love* that this is past tense! Aren't you glad that it is past tense to God?

If Jesus had not come and lived a perfect life for us and then died for us and then rose for us, then this statement would have to be "You *are* dead in your offenses and sins." Can you imagine if God was saying that about us?

But Jesus *did* do all of that for us! Because Paul is talking to the Ephesian church and to Christians, he is referring to their state of being dead in the past tense—as it is also past tense for all of us who have agreed to become set apart for God. Therefore, we *were* dead in the past, but we aren't any longer! Paul circles back around to explain this further in a few more verses.

(Quick reminder: There actually is someone—our spiritual enemy and our accuser—who tries to convince us that we are still dead in our sin. First, he tries to convince people that they aren't really dead apart from Jesus. But once a person knows it and accepts salvation, then he works to make us think we're *still* dead! Realizing this can help us to clearly identify the voices that are trying to speak into our mind and emotions.)

As we continue reading, notice the contrast between all of the wonderful truths that we can access because we are in Him compared to what we *used* to be. **Remember that the past tense that I'm referencing is past *in God's timeline*!**

Don't make the mistake of looking at your life in our natural timeline and getting yourself all confused because some sin seems to be in your "present." Just take God's Word for it!

No matter what you see in your life with your natural eyes, and no matter what you understand with your natural mind, **God says your sin is all past tense.** When Jesus died, He said, "It is **finished**!" Not "It has begun."

~~~~~~~~~~
John 19:30
He said, "It is finished!" And He bowed His head and gave up His spirit.
~~~~~~~~~~

Praise the Lord; it is finished!

The more you choose to believe this, the more you'll actually see it in your life because faith—your choice to believe what He says—is what releases God to work in you and transform your mind. Your actions and your life will naturally follow as His Spirit flows in you more and more.

~~~~~~~~~~
Romans 12:2
And do not be conformed to this world, but be transformed by the renewing of your mind, so that you may prove what the will of God is, that which is good and acceptable and perfect.
~~~~~~~~~~

And the more His Spirit flows, the more you'll see the fruit of *Him* and the less you'll see the fruit of *you*!

~~~~~~~~~~
Galatians 5:16
But I say, walk by the Spirit, and you will not carry out the desire of the flesh... 18 But if you are led by the Spirit, you are not under the Law. 22 But the fruit of the Spirit is love, joy, peace, patience, kindness, goodness, faithfulness, 23 gentleness, self-control; against such things there is no law.
~~~~~~~~~~

Writing Prompt
Is this *real* to you that you *were* dead but aren't anymore? If you struggle with this, then take a few minutes and write out your struggles to God. Be honest with your heart and what You desire Him to reveal to you. This honesty is faith, and it makes Him smile.

Paul goes on to talk about more about this death:

~*~ **Eph 2:2 in which you previously walked according to the course of this world, according to the prince of the power of the air, of the spirit that is now working in the sons of disobedience.**

Here is past tense again! We *previously* walked from God's point of view. Because now we aren't walking by ourselves—we are <u>in Him</u>!

Again, it's important to recognize this. The reality is that recognizing *what we would be without Jesus* is the starting point to accepting Him. This is the only true reason for accepting Him—because we know what we are without Him. You've missed the mark if you prayed "the sinner's prayer" because somebody scared you about hell or because your friends did. We **must** realize *why* we need Him!

The verse says we walked "according to the course of this world." This references the fact that the ways of the world are the ways of death. This is not a statement of condemnation against the things that non-Christians do. *That is looking at it backwards, as if the things that non-Christians do bring death.*

No, sin and death entered the world when Adam sinned, because Adam's decision to sin gave the devil permission to work on the earth. **Now sin and death simply *are* the way of the world.** It is now *natural* to walk in sin and death—unless you have been saved and redeemed out of it by Jesus!

To me, this distinction is very important! If we think that people's sinful actions lead to death, then it is very easy to fall into judgmental mindsets about those people. If, however, we recognize that it's the other way around and that they sin *because* sin and death are in the world, then we can have compassion on them like Jesus did. We can really love them.

~~~~~~~~~~
Matthew 9:36
Seeing the crowds, He felt compassion for them, because they were distressed and downcast, like sheep without a shepherd.
~~~~~~~~~~

Paul clarifies this as well. He says that "the course of this world" that he's talking about is the one that is "according to the prince of the power of the air" and "the spirit that is now working in the sons of disobedience." Both "the prince" and "the spirit" refer to the devil and the spiritual forces of evil.

~*~ **Eph 2:3 Among them we too all previously lived in the lusts of our flesh, indulging the desires of the flesh and of the mind, and were by nature children of wrath, just as the rest.**

Here Paul explains why we need to understand the death that sin caused, and he talks a little more about what that looks like.

What are the lusts of the flesh? To me, there are two main categories: *evil desires* and *desires that are out of balance*.

Evil desires

Some evil desires are pretty easy for most Christians to identify because our "Christian culture" doesn't accept them: Drugs, illicit sex, pornography, the high that comes from theft, lies (which satisfy the flesh when we think they protect us in some way).

Other evil desires are more subtle, and unfortunately, our Christian culture has accepted some of these to the point that sometimes those outside our culture looking in are more aware of the sin than we are. Some examples that God has opened my own eyes to are pride, gossip, strife, selfishness, and haughtiness.

Desires that are out of balance

But then there are desires which are sometimes natural and even healthy, but which can become out of balance to the point where we have a lust for them. This is the difference between a *desire* of our body or mind and a *lust* of our body or mind.

These are often the most difficult to surrender for those of us who have been Christians for a long time! Let's talk about some examples to make sure that we are correctly identifying this balance.

The desire for food is a natural desire that God created our body to have. But sometimes the desire for food gains the wrong place in our life. When we are struggling with feeling down, God calls us to draw upon Him because He is the lifter of our head.

~~~~~~~~~
Psalm 3:3
But You, Lord, are a shield around me,
My glory, and the One who lifts my head.
~~~~~~~~~

But if instead we turn to food for comfort, then we open ourselves up to the sin of gluttony which is a lust of the flesh. This is when food becomes a lust of the flesh. Notice it's the *heart status* that's different, not the particular food being eaten, when, where, or how much.

Rest is another example. Rest is so important that God set an example for us by resting on the seventh day. But what about when we abandon time with God or the things that He is calling us to do and *instead* spend that time sleeping or playing on our phones or reading or whatever it is that we like to do for rest? This is when rest becomes a lust of the flesh!

Isaiah talks about how we actually gain strength from spending time with God. This means that physical rest is *never* a substitute for time with God.

~~~~~~~~~~
Isaiah 40:31
Yet those who wait for the Lord will gain new strength;
They will mount up with wings like eagles,
They will run and not get tired,
They will walk and not become weary.
~~~~~~~~~~

I'm not saying that rest isn't important! It definitely is! But our rest needs to be tied to God's presence and seeking Him. The rest that we find with Him will far surpass what we'll find on a vacation or in several hours of surfing the Internet or watching TV.

Notice that neither sleep nor reading nor watching TV nor using our phones are sins in and of themselves. Sleep is necessary and important, and reading and using our phones can be relaxing and useful and enriching (depending on what we're reading and using them for). TV can be used in enriching ways too. Yet they can become a lust of the flesh *when we turn to them for stress-relief*, instead of spending time with the One who promised to renew our strength.

The desire for "things" is often okay. "There are needs, and then there are wants" is a well-known saying, but God is a loving Father who often delights in giving us things that are wants (or giving us the money to buy some). However, when we start thinking that our "wants" are actually "needs" and we are not content without them, then we are dealing with another lust of the flesh.

It makes no difference whether we have the money to purchase the thing we want or not. I remember once when I had the money to get something, and God stopped me by saying, "That's not what I gave you that money for." He desired me to give that money somewhere, but my flesh wanted to spend that money on clothes that I didn't actually need. Yet after that, there were times when I found a pretty piece of clothing and prayed, "Father, is it okay if I spend this money You gave me on this?" And I felt His peace and love surround me, telling me that yes, He was pleased to give me the means of purchasing that item.

God wants us to learn what Paul learned when he said that he had learned the secret of being content both when he was in need and when he had plenty. This is tied with more verses later in the same chapter, when he reminded the Philippians that God would supply their needs.

~~~~~~~~~

Philippians 4:12
I know how to get along with little, and I also know how to live in prosperity; in any and every circumstance I have learned the secret of being filled and going hungry, both of having abundance and suffering need.

~~~~~~~~~

I believe that Paul was content when he was in need because he knew that God *would* meet that need, and he was content when he was in plenty because he knew that God *had* supplied his needs. It was the same trust and reliance upon God either way, and it did not matter to him if God supplied the need last minute or whether God supplied it in advance!

Remember again, though—when we see a lust of the flesh in our lives, the solution is *not* to try harder to avoid it! The solution is to realize that this is a fruit of the flesh, and it will disappear and be replaced by the fruit of the Spirit, the more God transforms us so that His Spirit can flow through us! So we say, "Ugh, here is a lust of the flesh. Jesus, thank You that You died for me! Father, I'm here to seek You because I know that the closer I draw to You, the more You will give me life-changing revelations. I want my life to show the fruit of the Spirit instead of the fruit of the flesh, so here I am! I'm Yours!"

A big part of walking with God is allowing His Spirit to convict us when things are out of balance in our lives. He always does this because He wants what's best for us, and He doesn't want us to continue on paths that are stealing from our future!

Writing Prompts

I want to encourage you now to ask God to show you two things.
1. Ask Him what lusts of the flesh are still holding you back.
2. But then ask Him to reveal to you the victory over them that Jesus died for! It's not enough to just know in your head that Jesus died for them. It's *revelation* that changes us! It's His *grace* that empowers us to live in the freedom that Jesus died for! I am *not* encouraging you to embark on a plan of human effort to overcome whatever is holding you back. If you could do that, then Jesus wouldn't have had to die! But He *did* die, because He knew that His death was the *only* way that we could be free!

_____

_____

_____

_____

_____

_____

_____

_____

_____

_____

Now that Paul has reminded us that who and what we were before Christ is no different than that of the world around us, he goes on to talk some *more* about what Jesus did for us!

~*~ Eph 2:4 But God, being rich in mercy, because of His great love with which He loved us,

"But God" is a phrase that Christians like to use, and I think maybe we got it from this verse!

First Paul states the *why* here in this verse, before he even gets into what God actually did. He's saying, "All right. We all know what we used to be. This is who God is. I want to make sure you realize that what God did for us isn't because we did anything to deserve it. It's purely because of who He is. He is rich in mercy, and He loves us so very, very, very much!"

~*~ Eph 2:5 even when we were dead in our wrongdoings,

Those words "even when" mean that God took the first move. He didn't wait for us to call on Him first. He didn't wait for us to try really hard.
We were *dead* when He made His move.
Thank God that He didn't wait for us!

Paul is now going to list three things that God did.

~*~ Eph 2: (v.5 continued) …[He] made us alive together with Christ (by grace you have been saved),

This is the first thing Paul lists: God brought us back to life spiritually!
That parenthetical note at the end is a quick reminder that this resurrection power that God puts to work here is called **His grace.** All of the things that Jesus did to save us and that He does in our lives now are actions carried out by the power of His grace.

~*~ Eph 2:6 and raised us up with Him,

This is the second thing Paul lists. Note the word "with" that he used in both of these last two statements. It means that our resurrection from this place of spiritual death to a place of spiritual life happened *when Jesus rose from the dead.*

How is this possible? If someone is saved today, this is almost 2,000 years after Jesus rose from the dead! Ah, but remember that God exists outside of time. He is not limited by time. Something that happened thousands of years ago and something that happened fifteen days ago can both be happening at the same time to God!

This is hard to wrap our minds around, yet God says it is so! His word, right here in this verse, says that we who are living now in the 21st century and who have set ourselves apart for Him *were raised*—past tense—up with Jesus!

Remember everything the first chapter said about how we are <u>in Christ Jesus</u>? When we agree with Him that we are "set apart" for Him, then God, working from outside time, rearranges the spiritual DNA of our life. Just as the earliest existence of your physical body was alive inside your grandmother before she was born, so the existence of your spiritual self was placed <u>in Christ</u> when He rose from the dead!

If this was a time travel movie, we'd say that God went back in time to insert you into Jesus, thus immediately changing the trajectory of your life in irrevocable ways. But since He is outside of time, He doesn't have to time-travel to do exactly that!

~*~ Eph 2: (v.6 continued) ...and seated us with Him in the heavenly places in Christ Jesus,

Paul finishes up these statements of what God *did in the past* with his third statement, which also establishes *where we are right now*, spiritually. We *are* seated with God, because that is where Jesus is, and we are in Him!

Hebrews says that after Jesus did His work of purification for us (by dying and rising again), He sat down at the right hand of the Father, in heaven.

~~~~~~~~~
Hebrews 1:3
When He had made purification of sins, He sat down at the right hand of the Majesty on high...
~~~~~~~~~

So this is where *we* are right now, spiritually, from the point of view of God, our Father. Yes, He knows our spiritual bodies are here on earth, and our minds struggle with our understanding of life on earth and how all these spiritual truths fit in. But He's up there, with Jesus at His right hand, and to Him, *we are in Jesus.*

~*~ Eph 2:7 so that in the ages to come He might show the boundless riches of His grace in kindness toward us in Christ Jesus.

Now that Paul has listed the three things that Jesus did, he explains God's goal for doing all this. His love for us prompted Him to send Jesus (v. 4), and His end goal, explained here, is *to demonstrate grace and kindness toward us!*

Isn't He amazing? His nature has no selfishness. He just wants to give and give and give to His people.

These next two verses are some of the most quoted in Christianity, but I want to break them down and consider carefully what they're saying. Sometimes the verses that are most familiar to us can be taken for granted. Sometimes we just skim them, thinking, "Oh, I know that one." It's like when we say we know how our phone works because we can work the buttons and touchscreen, even though we really have no idea exactly how the phone can tell the touch of our fingers apart from the touch of our pocket, and then turn that touch (or two or three simultaneously) into a command for a program to execute a certain action that is then displayed on that same screen!

This next verse explains how God actually designed salvation to "work." So let's look at it!

~*~ Eph 2:8 For by grace you have been saved through faith; and this is not of yourselves, it is the gift of God;

Let's think of what the word "by" means in this context. Miriam-Websters dictionary lists many definitions for the word "by," but the one that's being employed here is "through the agency of." It's the same as when the Pharisees asked Jesus, "*By* what authority do you work these miracles?" Or when we say that something was taken *by* force.

So here, Paul is saying we are saved *by* grace.

Of course, we know we were saved by Jesus, so is this a contradiction? Or is Paul trying to explain something more about everything the last few verses were recounting? Something about grace?

What is grace? Often we talk about grace as if it is the same thing as mercy—not receiving a deserved punishment. But grace and mercy are not the same thing! Grace is connected to mercy, for we could never receive God's grace unless He first extended His mercy. But it's more than that. **Grace is God's enabling *power* flowing by His Spirit through a human.**

Many verses talk about grace and demonstrate this tie between grace and supernatural power, activated in our lives.

God told Paul this:

~~~~~~~~~
2 Corinthians 12:9
My **grace** is sufficient for you,
for **power** is perfected in weakness.
~~~~~~~~~

In other words, It's His Spirit making it possible for a human to fulfill His will in a way that would otherwise not be possible.

Grace is when God calls you to do something you could never be capable of doing yourself, and then He works in such a way that you do it anyway, except you know it wasn't you.

That is God's grace at work!

When Luke wrote the book of Acts, quite a few times he included the link between power and grace.

Acts 4:33
And with **great power** the apostles were giving testimony to the resurrection of the Lord Jesus, and **abundant grace** was upon them all.

Luke recounted in chapters ten and eleven how Barnabas saw that the gift of tongues had been poured out on Gentiles for the first time. Luke described it by saying that Barnabas was witnessing the grace of God. In other words, he witnessed God empowering humans to do what they could not do on their own.

Later on, Luke mentions that more miracles were happening and again linked the supernatural power that was flowing to grace. These signs and wonders were nothing they could do in their own power!

Acts 14:3
[God was] testifying to **the word of His grace**, granting that **signs and wonders** be performed by their hands.

Paul also talked about how grace empowers us:

~~~~~~~~~~
Romans 5:2
Through whom [Jesus] we also have obtained our introduction by faith into **this grace in which we stand**.
~~~~~~~~~~

Paul also talks about how we have different gifts, because the grace—empowering—given to each of us is different.

~~~~~~~~~~
Romans 12:6
However, since we have gifts that differ **according to the grace given to us**, each of us is to use them properly: if prophecy, in proportion to one's faith;
~~~~~~~~~~

Paul also explained to Timothy that our calling is not according to our works. God doesn't decide our calling based on what we're capable of doing with human ability and strength. Our calling is according to God's purpose and His grace. It's according to what He wants to achieve on the earth through us, which He then empowers us to do through His Spirit.

~~~~~~~~~~
2 Timothy 1:9
[God] who saved us and called us with a holy calling, not according to our works, but according to His own purpose and grace, which was granted to us in Christ Jesus from all eternity,
~~~~~~~~~~

All of these verses talk about ways that He empowers us, but the first extension of His grace toward us is when He saved us. That's what the first few words of this verse in Ephesians are saying. It's *by the empowering of His Spirit* that He saved us.

But then this verse in Ephesians says it is also "through faith!"

This is yet another facet of how salvation "works." God extends His grace—the power of His Spirit—toward us and enables us to believe something that we could not otherwise believe. **This is faith.** It is the channel we're given to receive *everything* that He desires to give us, starting with salvation itself.

If it were not for His Spirit giving us the power/ability to believe in faith, then we could never believe that we are "in" someone who walked the earth 2,000 years ago, and that His death and resurrection changes our lives today. That's why Paul tries to make it extra clear, saying, "This is not your own doing. This was God's gift to you!"

So therefore, we could explain this verse in this way: "I am saved because God, through His Spirit, extended His power to touch my life. He gave me the ability to believe something that I could never hope to understand otherwise—that He saved me by sending Jesus."

Writing Prompt

What does this verse mean to you? Does this deepen your understanding of salvation?

_____

_____

_____

_____

_____

_____

The next verse continues the same thought, explaining how our salvation is received. Paul is essentially saying the same thing to try to make it extra clear:

~*~ Eph 2:9 not a result of works, so that no one may boast.

This little verse is a reflection back to Romans chapter three where Paul went into great detail explaining that the purpose of the Law was to show us that we *couldn't* save ourselves through our own actions. It never has been possible and never will be possible!

~~~~~~~~~~
Romans 3:20
...because by the works of the Law none of mankind will be justified in His sight; for through the Law comes knowledge of sin.
~~~~~~~~~~

We'll talk about this more in a few pages when we get down to verse 15.

~*~ Eph 2:10 For we are His workmanship,

I love this statement that we are His workmanship, for **God is a craftsman**. Many years ago, I had a conversation with my brother that really illuminated this verse to me.

We were talking about God working in people, and how it's always a process. We talked about how God has to often remind us of things He's shown us in the past. Sometimes He has to re-reveal things to me because we tend to forget as time goes by.

My brother mentioned how today's society is a results-oriented society. We attend classes and receive training, and once we've been through it once, we're expected to produce results. And he's right. The vast majority of our culture is indeed that way.

The problem is that we tend to figure that God must be that way, too. We think that if He's shown us something once and it doesn't produce immediate, permanent change in our lives, then we've failed Him.

We sometimes think that this means that He's given up on us. Or maybe we think that He's altered His plan for our lives because we're not measuring high enough for His original purpose. Sometimes we think that that grace can't possibly overcome the anger that He must be feeling over the fact that we've failed Him so many times.

But at that point, my brother pointed out that God isn't a businessman or a mass-producer. What is He? He is a *craftsman*.

Think of it! What does a dedicated craftsman do? Is he concerned with how fast he produces his masterpiece? No! Is he concerned with how much time and work it takes to perfect it? Not really!

What concerns a craftsman the most is the finished product. His main desire is that it become what He intended it to be. If it's not, then He patiently works away, whittling away, or adding, or shaping, dedicating as much time as is needed to get it right.

And so it is with us. "For we are His workmanship."

Writing Prompt
What does this mean to you?

_____
_____
_____
_____
_____
_____
_____
_____
_____
_____
_____
_____
_____
_____
_____
_____
_____
_____
_____
_____

Are you wondering why God would spend so much time perfecting His craftsmanship in you? This is why:

~*~ **Eph 2:10 (continued)** ...created in Christ Jesus for good works, which God prepared beforehand so that we would walk in them.

Let's think for a minute of how this part of the verse would sound if a human father said it. "Yeah, I've got a list of all the things my son—who hasn't been conceived yet—is going to do." We'd look at him like he was crazy! How does he know what his son will or won't be able to do?

The reality is that he doesn't. He can make plans in what to teach his son, and he can have hopes and dreams. But he cannot change his son's natural abilities.

But since God's plans include *empowering us by His grace*, then God can certainly make such plans!

The fact that we are now "in Christ Jesus" is also part of why/how God could make such plans for us before we were created. Read this passage:

~~~~~~~~~

Psalm 139:13
For You created my innermost parts;
You wove me in my mother's womb.
14 I will give thanks to You,
because I am awesomely and wonderfully made;
Wonderful are Your works,
And my soul knows it very well.
15 My frame was not hidden from You
When I was made in secret,
And skillfully formed in the depths of the earth;
16 Your eyes have seen my formless substance;
And in Your book were written
All the days that were ordained for me,
When as yet there was not one of them.

~~~~~~~~~

God knows everything about our lives. He knows the choices that we will make. Before we were conceived, He already knew the schedule He was going to follow as He worked on us as a Craftsman.

This is how and why God was able to prepare good works for us before time began.

Does this humble you as it does me? Are you realizing how very, very dependent upon God's grace you are for doing anything that's really, truly *worth doing?*

I hope you also feel *valued*, knowing that God is a craftsman, and *you* are one of His masterpieces!

Writing Prompt
I encourage you to spend a bit of time talking with God about this. Let Him show you how He sees you!

~*~ **Eph 2:11 Therefore remember that previously you, the Gentiles in the flesh, who are called "Uncircumcision" by the so-called "Circumcision" which is performed in the flesh by human hands— 12 remember that you were at that time separate from Christ, excluded from the people of Israel, and strangers to the covenants of the promise, having no hope and without God in the world. 13 But now in Christ Jesus you who previously were far away have been brought near by the blood of Christ.**

The references to circumcision refer to the division between the Jews and Gentiles.

In the Old Testament and according to the Jewish law, circumcision was the physical sign that you were of Israel—that you were one of God's people. So here, Paul reminds the Ephesians that before Christ—before they were supernaturally placed "in Him"—they were not one of God's people because they were not Jews. *Now they are in Christ Jesus.*

Before they had no hope. *Now they do.*

The new not only replaced the old; *it's superior*.

The previous covenant (that excluded them) had the sign of *a changed body through circumcision*. The sign of the new covenant is *a changed life*.

~~~~~~~~~

Matthew 7:16
You will know them by their fruits.

~~~~~~~~~

John 13:35
By this all people will know that you are My disciples: if you have love for one another.

~~~~~~~~~

~*~ **Eph 2:14 For He Himself is our peace, who made both groups into one and broke down the barrier of the dividing wall,**

Here in this verse, Paul shows the new reality that came about because of Jesus.

Both Jews and Gentiles are now one in Him. *Both* have been brought near to God, and not in two separate ways. They have been brought near *together* as one group now.

~*~ **Eph 2:15 by abolishing in His flesh the hostility, which is the Law composed of commandments expressed in ordinances, so that <u>in Himself</u> He might** make the two one new person, in this way establishing peace; 16 and that He might reconcile them both in one body to God through the cross, by it having put to death the hostility. 17 And He came and preached peace to you who were far away, and peace to those who were near; 18 for through Him we both have our access in one Spirit to the Father.

These two verses continue talking about the two-who-have-been-made-one, but now Paul is also talking about another separation that was healed—the one between humans and God.

Verse 14 said that Jesus is our peace, and verse 15 says that this is because He abolished a certain hostility—hostility being an opposite of peace. But Paul says that what he means by "hostility" is the Law. In other words, hostility is all the rules and regulations which the Jews were under.

How is the Law hostility? To understand this, we need to look at a section of Romans.

~~~~~~~~~~
Romans 3:20
...because by the works of the Law none of mankind will be justified in His sight; for through the Law comes knowledge of sin.
~~~~~~~~~~

God did give the Law, but Romans 3 explains that the law was given *to explain what sin was*. In other words, God was wanting to explain to humans what would harm them and what separates them from Him.

But God always intended the law to be merely the first part of His plan. Hebrews explains that even though the Law was given, *even then*, for those who lived daily with the Law, their *actual* righteousness was faith. It was their willingness to believe that if they obeyed God and sacrificed this lamb for their sins, that God granted forgiveness. It wasn't that all those lambs were *actually* paying for their sin. Not like Jesus did on the cross. It was an act of obedience and symbol of their faith, and *that* is what pleased God.

~~~~~~~~~
Hebrews 11:1
Now faith is the certainty of things hoped for, a proof of things not seen. 2 For **by it the people of old gained approval.**
~~~~~~~~~

God's plan all along was for the Gentiles to be His as well. Isaiah 49 is prophetic—Jesus is speaking through the Spirit of God, many years before He entered our timeline.

~~~~~~~~~
Isaiah 49:5
And now says the Lord, who formed
Me from the womb to be His Servant,
To bring Jacob back to Him,
so that Israel might be gathered to Him ...
6 He says, "It is too small a thing that
You should be My Servant
To raise up the tribes of Jacob and
to restore the protected ones of Israel;
I will also make You a light of the nations
So that <u>My salvation</u> may reach to the end of the earth."
~~~~~~~~~

God said it's too small a thing for Him to *only* bring the people of Israel to Himself. His intention is for His salvation to reach the ends of the earth! (Awesome little side note—in the Hebrew, those two words "My salvation" are the word "Yeshua" which was Jesus's name in Hebrew.)

And yet, despite all this, Paul—a teacher and expert of the law—calls the Law hostility, twice in these two verses of Ephesians!

I believe He is referring to the same thing he talked about in Romans when he essentially said, "If it hadn't been for the law, I wouldn't have known what sin was. But now I know, and woe is me!"

If we think of our American phrase, "Ignorance is bliss," it can help us understand this.

Consider a person who grew up in poverty in a third world country, with very few opportunities. They were isolated enough from the outside world, however, that they didn't know how poor their culture was. It was normal to grow up and learn the trade of your father, to struggle and go hungry sometimes, to lose family members to disease, and to celebrate the days you did have with your loved ones.

Then they found out about the outside world. They learned that there are people who never go hungry, who rarely lose loved ones to disease, and who get to choose the trade that they want to learn. Suddenly, this person is no longer satisfied with the life they had for so long. Now they know how much more is actually possible.

In this example, the person was happier before they found out how much more was out there, and so we might be tempted to think they were better off not knowing.

But what if we consider a third state—one of *having* the "more?" What if they were given the opportunity to bring their family to a better place, where hunger became a thing of the past, medicine was able to save their family members who had been dying, and education made any trade possible?

Wouldn't that be better yet?

Of course it is!

Now consider this: If they had never discovered that more existed, would they have reached out for it?

No.

It's the same way with us. In order for us to actually reach out for more, we first have to be made aware of its existence. This creates a dissatisfaction within us where we were once happy… which then prompts us to reach out for more… which we then receive.

In the case of God, there is also the factor of *His* desires. We might have thought we were happy without Him, but *He wasn't happy apart from us*. And of course, because He created us, He knew that whatever happiness we thought we had without Him, it was nothing compared to what we could have <u>with Him.</u>

So it is this middle state, of discovering a lack, that the Law represented. It brought the Jews closer to God (compared to the Gentiles) by making them aware of what they did not have and giving them a temporary (in our timeline) way of reaching out to God. But the law did not make it possible for them to be <u>in Him</u>.

So what Jesus did on the cross was that He took care of both things at the same time. He completed what had been the plan all along, to bring the Jews to the Father <u>in Himself</u> and bring the Gentiles <u>in Himself</u> as well!

God revealed that His plan all along was for the Gentiles to be "<u>in Christ</u>" as well. A metaphor might be to say that the Jews were the example, but anyone could learn from that example.

And then of course, because there is no division <u>in Christ Jesus</u>, we understand that if both Jews and Gentile believers are now <u>in Him</u>, then of course there can be no division within them anymore either!

~*~ Eph 2:19 So then you are no longer strangers and foreigners, but you are fellow citizens with the saints, and are of God's household,

This is Paul's summary of the whole section. He's circling around everything yet again, using slightly different metaphors and images this time.

According to this metaphor, the Gentiles were strangers and foreigners, while the Jews were citizens... and yet now those who believe are not just citizens, they are of God's household!

~*~ Eph 2:20 having been built on the foundation of the apostles and prophets, Christ Jesus Himself being the cornerstone, 21 <u>in whom</u> the whole building, being fitted together, is growing into a holy temple <u>in the Lord</u>,

Notice how many times the words <u>in Him</u> are still being used!

Here we have yet another metaphor and picture of constructing a building to help us understand.

We can't think of modern building methods, which Paul was unaware of. We must consider ancient building methods which used stones for foundations. The cornerstone was the first stone laid. Then the next were laid next to it, and so forth. Consider how, if that first tone was laid crooked—perhaps twisted a little to the south—then as the next and the next were laid, that line would continue to the south, farther and farther. So if the first stone was twisted to the south just the tiniest bit, then by the time you got to the other end of the house, it would be much farther off! Or what if one side of that cornerstone was higher than the other? <u>Either</u> the next stone would not sit flush against it, or else it too would have to be crooked.

This is why the cornerstone is so important. Here Paul refers to the apostles and prophets as the foundation. This is because these were the first messengers God sent to preach. In the Old Testament, we had prophets calling people to God, prophesying what God was going to do to hint at the whole big picture, even though they were only in the middle stage of the law.

Then the apostles in the New Testament were chosen by Jesus to be taught by Him and to walk with Him so that when the Holy Spirit came, He could explain everything fully.

~~~~~~~~~
John 14:25
"These things I have spoken to you while remaining with you. 26 But the Helper, the Holy Spirit whom the Father will send in My name, He will teach you all things, and remind you of all that I said to you."
~~~~~~~~~

Then *they* were given the mission to tell the world!

So here, Jesus is the cornerstone that was laid first, and then the prophets and apostles are the rest of the foundation.

And then Paul says that we who are in Him are the rest of the building! Paul describes the building as a temple (which was their holy building at the time), but this is no different than us today, referring to ourselves as the church.

~~~~~~~~~
1 Peter 2:5
You also, as living stones, are being built up as a spiritual house for a holy priesthood, to offer spiritual sacrifices that are acceptable to God through Jesus Christ.
~~~~~~~~~

We go to church—the building which is "set apart" (holy) for worshiping Him and coming together. But we also say that the church isn't really a building, it's the people. This passage is explaining why we talk about ourselves this way.

~*~ **Eph 2:22 in whom you also are being built together into a dwelling of God <u>in the Spirit</u>.**

Finally, Paul again circles back to how, even though we are <u>in Him</u>, He is also in us through His Spirit. We, the church, are His dwelling place here on earth.

This was God's intention all along. As far back as the book of Isaiah, God said, "Who am I that I can dwell in a building?"

~~~~~~~~~~
Isaiah 66:1
This is what the Lord says: "Heaven is My throne and the earth is the footstool for My feet. Where then is a house you could build for Me? And where is a place that I may rest?
~~~~~~~~~~

I find it totally amazing that God created us in such a way that He could dwell in us!

Writing Prompt

As we finish this chapter, reflect on what it means to you to have God dwell <u>in you</u>. Write out whatever is on your heart the most and let Him speak words of affirmation and love and grace into your life!

_____

_____

_____

_____

_____

Chapter Three

Chapter two left off with Paul's reminder of how everyone who believes—both Jews and Gentiles—is now both in Christ *and* is the dwelling place of God.

In the beginning of *this* chapter, the focus is still on this world-changing idea that Jesus did not come only to save those who had Jewish blood. He came to save the world! Paul also talks more about our calling in this chapter.

Paul starts out talking about how his calling was to preach this world-changing truth.

~*~ Eph 3:1 For this reason I, Paul, the prisoner of Christ Jesus for the sake of you Gentiles

"For this reason" refers to what Paul was just saying in chapter two. Remember that this was a letter he wrote, and it wasn't divided into chapters. To him, this was a continuation of thought.

So he's saying essentially, "Everything that I just explained (in chapter two) is the reason that..." In other words, he wouldn't be doing the preaching and writing and whatever he's about to talk about next if it weren't for the truths (for Gentiles) that he was just referencing in chapter two.

He also references the fact that he was a prisoner when he was writing this. This little statement here tells us that Paul wrote this letter while he was imprisoned in Rome.

It's quite interesting that Paul calls himself the prisoner *of Christ Jesus*, instead of the prisoner of the Romans or the prisoner of Nero. Nero would have said Paul was his prisoner, but Paul doesn't identify himself that way.

I believe he identified himself as a prisoner of Christ Jesus because he considered his life totally surrendered to God. In his mind, it wasn't really up to Nero what happened to him. It was up to God. He was in chains because of God's will, not Nero's.

He also says that he's a prisoner "for the sake of the Gentiles." This is a little hard to understand, but let's keep reading and come back to this phrase because at the end of this verse, Paul interrupts himself and circles away to explain this "for the sake of you Gentiles" statement. (He'll come back to continue his "for this reason" statement in verse 14.)

~*~ Eph 3:2 if indeed you have heard of the administration of God's grace which was given to me for you;

The word "you" here refers to the Gentiles. Remember that he is writing to a Gentile church, and he just finished reminding them, as Gentiles, that they were brought near through Christ Jesus.

His words "if indeed" indicate that delineation or condition. He's sending this letter to the church of Ephesus, but he knows that there may be people hearing or reading this letter who are not (yet) in Christ and part of His body and the dwelling place of God's Spirit. He also knows that this letter might be heard by some people who don't really know who he, Paul, is. Perhaps they don't know why they can trust these things that he's writing. So these words "if indeed" indicate to us the direction of this circle that he's making. He's clarifying that the whole reason he is sending them this letter, and why he preaches what he does, is because this is the grace—the anointing and calling—that God gave him.

Paul is determined to be faithful to the calling and not to waste the grace—the empowering—that God gave him.

How about you?

Do you know what your calling is? We often talk about "a calling" as if it's just one thing, but most of the time our calling is multi-faceted. It also often shifts with the seasons of our life.

Remember that a calling isn't always something with a title we can label. My mom's calling included reaching out to people, encouraging them, and making them feel seen and valued. I'm not sure if she ever realized that this was her calling and what she was anointed for, but it was very evident at her funeral, when hundreds and hundreds of people came because of the encouraging impact she had made on their lives.

Regardless of whether you do know what your calling is or don't know, the question that really matters is this: **how deep is your desire to be faithful to what God is calling you to do?**

Notice that *I do not ask how well you are doing it*. Living for God is not about *man's* definitions of success—even ministry success! Living for God is about abiding in Him and *willingness* to go when He says go and stay when He says stay, minute by minute and day by day. **God cannot lead us to where He wants to take us in our future if we're not willing to walk with Him in obedience in our here-and-now.**

It's about obedience more than achievement! True obedience starts in the heart, and that is why I ask about *the depth of your desire to be faithful.*

~~~~~~~~~~

Matthew 15:18

"But the things that come out of the mouth come from the heart, and those things defile the person. 19 For out of the heart come evil thoughts, murders, acts of adultery, other immoral sexual acts, thefts, false testimonies, and slanderous statements. 20 These are the things that defile the person;"

~~~~~~~~~~

Jesus taught that how we live our daily life reflects the deepest desires of our hearts. Thus, our faithfulness to what God has called us to do will be the natural result of our heart's willingness, *regardless of whether or not our mind knows what He's actually calling us to do!*

Here is an example from my own life.

For many years, the employment of almost a hundred people depended on my faithfulness and wisdom in my job. But God did not tell me in advance that He was calling me to that. I would have been quite intimidated! I did not even realize the impact that my job had for quite a while after I was doing it. I simply prayed about a job offer I'd received to part-time editing, and as the years went by, I always did my best to follow God's leading because that was my desire. I strived to be faithful in each new responsibility that was given to me… and that is where I ended up. When I left that job, many people told me of the impact I had on their life, and I was quite surprised by some of the things they said!

When God opened the door for me to leave that job, it was again for a minor part-time job that appeared to not have much impact—and yet now, several years later, I'm once again in a pivotal position that indirectly impacts many people's lives. It doesn't appear to impact them *spiritually*, and sometimes I wonder why God actually has me here. My company has lofty goals of changing the world of the Internet, but I don't know if they'll succeed or how much God cares about their goals. But I am content to trust that He knows what He is doing and why He has me here, and I will follow where He leads no matter how baffling it might sometimes be.

So how deep is *your* desire to do what God has called you to do *today*? This week?

Often our willingness to follow His leading is tested by our coworkers and family and environment, and we're tempted to complain about where He has us this week.

Think about this:

> Our heart's willingness to
> go where He will call in the future
> is measured by our willingness to
> walk through whatever today holds.

That's not a scripture verse, but it's a reflection of what Jesus said when He told the parable of the servants with the talents.

~~~~~~~~~

Luke 16:10
"The one who is faithful in a very little thing is also faithful in much; and the one who is unrighteous in a very little thing is also unrighteous in much."

~~~~~~~~~

The reality is that our future consists of many individual steps that we will take, moment by moment and day by day.

Are you content to hold His hand and walk fearlessly and purposefully into your future, no matter how intimidating it is?

Are you willing to trust Him as you walk through today and tomorrow, no matter how meaningless and frustrating the steps you're taking right now appear to be? He might be touching other people's lives through yours right now, even though you can't see it!

You can be assured that the struggles you're going through now are preparing you for something in Your future that matters very much to Him and His kingdom!

Writing Prompt

I encourage you to talk with God about your hopes and fears and questions and desires and frustrations regarding whatever He has called you to do now. Then talk to Him about whatever callings might be unknown (to you) and in your future.

_____
_____
_____
_____
_____
_____
_____
_____
_____
_____
_____
_____
_____
_____
_____
_____
_____

Let's return to Ephesians, as Paul is talking about the grace and calling that he was given.

~*~ Eph 3:3 that by revelation there was made known to me the mystery, as I wrote before briefly.

By calling it a mystery, Paul is also saying that he *knows* that some of what he's talking about can be baffling! Actually, it's more than baffling. He's saying that it *cannot* be properly understood except by revelation from the Spirit of God.

This is a reminder that when we read something that makes us think, "Huh?" we shouldn't apply our *mind* to try to understand it. We should instead open our *spirit* to understand, asking the Holy Spirit to teach us the accurate truth. This is true of all scripture, not just Ephesians! For what Paul explains in the New Testament, the Holy Spirit taught him from the Old Testament, showing him God's intentions from the beginning of time and how they were fulfilled in Jesus!

~*~ Eph 3:4 By referring to this, when you read you can understand my insight into the mystery of Christ, 5 which in other generations was not made known to mankind, as it has now been revealed to His holy apostles and prophets in the Spirit;

Paul knew that this was "new." In the ancient world—and even many times today—what you are permitted to know and receive and be a part of is restricted according to race and birthright and nationality. This idea that the God "of the Jews" was calling *all* people was indeed very new, even though many of Paul's letters reference Old Testament prophecies indicating that this was God's intention all along. It was there, but they could not understand it.

If we combine all of the thoughts that Paul shares in the first five verses of this chapter, we can see that Paul is also wanting us, his readers, to understand that his insight regarding the mysteries of Christ *is because this is what God called him to share*. He was given these insights (and the grace/ empowerment to preach despite the cost) because this was his calling.

Sometimes we get this backwards. When we think of callings, sometimes we think that we could never do ____ (fill in the blank) because we can't ____. We think that what we can do for God is limited by our abilities. Maybe we *want* it to be like this because it's more comfortable that way.

But that's not how God works.

There's a popular Christian saying that goes something like this: "God doesn't call those who are equipped. He equips those He calls."

This is what Paul is trying to communicate in these last few verses. He wasn't called to share these world-changing revelations because his training as a Pharisee gave him an unusually thorough knowledge of the scriptures. This was his natural mind's ability, and we all know how *that* resulted in his former life's ambition to imprison and kill as many Christians as he could!

~~~~~~~~~~

Acts 22:3
"I am a Jew, born in Tarsus of Cilicia, but brought up in this city, educated under Gamaliel, strictly according to the Law of our fathers, being zealous for God just as you all are today. 4 I persecuted this Way to the death, binding and putting both men and women into prisons..."

~~~~~~~~~~

No! Paul was called to preach the Gospel to the Gentiles, *and therefore* God stepped in and gave him what he did *not* have— revelation and insight into what he never before understood.

So it is with us. God is busy giving us the revelations that we need for what He's *already* called us to do in our future. The best preparation we can make is to focus on learning to abide in Him!

~~~~~~~~~
John 15:4
"Remain in Me, and I in you. Just as the branch cannot bear fruit of itself but must remain in the vine, so neither can you unless you remain in Me."
~~~~~~~~~

~*~ Eph 3:6 to be specific, that the Gentiles are fellow heirs and fellow members of the body, and fellow partakers of the promise in Christ Jesus through the gospel, 7 of which I was made a minister, according to the gift of God's grace which was given to me according to the working of His power. 8 To me, the very least of all saints, this grace was given, to preach to the Gentiles the unfathomable riches of Christ,

Paul is closing the circle. Verse 6 sums up what the last chapter explained in detail, and verses 7 and 8 repeat Paul's acknowledgement that this was his calling… but only because God chose this as his calling… and he was only able to fulfill it because of God's empowering grace.

Now we can understand a little better what he meant when he said that he was a prisoner "for the sake of the Gentiles."

Let's say that a woman had a new baby and we desire to give her some rest. We therefore offer to take care of her older two kids for a day so she can rest and recover. We would then say that we are caring for the children "for their mom's sake." Our motivation is to help the mother. On the other hand, what if another woman willfully abandoned their children on a street corner, pinning a note to their chest saying that she didn't want them anymore… and we found them. Then, if we cared for those children, we would be doing it for *their* sake.

So when Paul said that he was the prisoner of Christ Jesus for the sake of the Gentiles, I think he was saying that because of his calling, anything that happened to him in the pursuit of that calling was for the sake of the Gentiles.

A missionary going through hardships in a foreign country would say the same thing—that the hardships were all for the sake of the people they went to serve.

~*~ Eph 3:9 and to enlighten all people as to what the plan of the mystery is which for ages has been hidden in God, who created all things;

Now Paul takes his summary further into new territory that he hasn't covered yet. He mentions a mystery that "for ages" hasn't been understood. Yet the reason for not understanding hadn't been ignorance or stupidity. It was hidden in God. This means that God's time for humans to understand had not yet come.

But look at the first part—"to enlighten all people" about it! Therefore the time *had* come for it to no longer be hidden.

This verse is an encouraging reminder to us that God's timing affects our ability to understand things. Our accuser often likes to try to condemn us and make us feel like we "should" understand things sooner or faster or more. But here, Paul says that God "hides" things and then decides when it is time for those things to become revealed.

This is so liberating to me! My natural tendency used to be, when I was presented with something I didn't understand, to put my wits and my intelligence against it and try, try, try to understand it. Then I would get frustrated when I didn't. But now I know that when it comes to the things of God, the better way is to *rest* in Him and to say, "Father God, there is a mystery here in this verse that I know I don't fully understand. I would like to understand it because I know Your Word is true. Please teach me, Holy Spirit of God, and enlighten my spirit to understand. And thank You that You enable me to be patient until that time comes, because Your timing is perfect."

~*~ Eph 3:10 so that the multifaceted wisdom of God might now be made known through the church to the rulers and the authorities in the heavenly places.

Here's another "so that" statement, telling us that God had a reason for deciding that it was time for the mystery to no longer be hidden.

What was the reason? Because God wanted to release "a multifaceted wisdom." A wisdom that is deep and that has many dimensions and many truths.

The next part of this statement is amazing. This wisdom is to be made known *through* the church *to the rulers and authorities in the heavenly places.* The words "in the heavenly places" indicate that he's not talking about man's kings and dictators. He's talking about the spiritual realm.

We don't know all the details about this realm, but we know that there are hierarchies of leadership in them. 1 Thessalonians 4:1 refers to an archangel or chief of angels, and Jude 1:9 names Michael as at least one of them.

Daniel 12:1 calls Michael "the great prince who stands guard over the sons of Israel." Daniel 10:13 recounts how an angel appears to Daniel. This angel isn't named, but he calls Michael "one of the chief princes." This unnamed angel who was speaking to Daniel was evidently a warrior, for he also refers to "princes of Persia" who were fighting against him and stopping him until Michael came to help him fight these evil princes. So we see the Bible use the word "princes" to refer to both God's angels and to evil spiritual beings.

Furthermore, when Jesus was being arrested and Peter drew his sword to defend Him, Jesus told Peter He did not need to be defended, for He could easily ask for—and immediately receive—twelve legions of angels to defend Him. God is indeed the Lord of Hosts! He is the God of angel armies!

So while there's a lot we don't know about the spiritual realm, it does seem clear that when the Bible mentions rulers and authorities in heavenly places, it's referring to these princes.

This verse in Ephesians indicates that these spiritual beings—even those in authority—do not (or did not) understand this multifaceted wisdom of God! God's plan was never to tell them directly. Instead, His plan has been for them to understand it *through the church!*

There is a lot that I don't understand about this. I don't know if angels immediately understood this plan or if the revelation of it will not be completely revealed until the very end of earthly time when the church is completely mature and revealed and received as the bride of Christ. This statement in Ephesians seems to indicate that the angels at least started to understand.

I also don't know what this multifaceted wisdom includes, or what the full scope of it encompasses.

But I think it's fascinating to have a glimpse of how God has woven together His purposes and revelations between our earthly "natural" realm and the spiritual realm!

~*~ Eph 3:11 This was in accordance with the eternal purpose which He carried out in Christ Jesus our Lord, 12 in whom we have boldness and confident access through faith in Him.

Paul is still referencing the revelations though the church to the spiritual realm. Here he says again that this was *always* God's plan, to carry it out in Jesus.

This is extremely reassuring. When mankind sinned, we didn't mess up God's original plan. We aren't living in Plan B. God always knew, before people were even created, that Adam would allow sin into the world, and Jesus would have to die. But still, creating us as He did, with the capacity to sin (and even the natural tendency to do it for all of us born after Adam) was *still* the plan He chose. This was *still* His method to achieve "His eternal purpose" as this verse states.

But notice again that our part in this eternal purpose hinges upon the fact that we are in Jesus. This is why Paul started this letter out by going into detail about what us being in Him actually means. Here he reminds us that it is because of Jesus that we have boldness, and it is because of Jesus that we have access to God—and not just any access. *Confident* access!

He also reminds us that it is through faith. Faith is not a focus of Ephesians, but it is clear that many of the things Paul is discussing aren't things we can see with our natural eyes. Everything he's been talking about can only be understood and lived by faith. We have to extend our faith to trust and believe all these things:

That God is who He says He is.

That He knows what He's talking about.

That He has done what He says He did.

That He is able to do what He says He will do.

That He will finish what He started in each of us.

That His Spirit will teach us what we need to understand and give us the revelations we need.

Writing Prompt

Spend a little bit of time with this list. Thank God for the things that He has already enabled you to totally *know* and rest in and believe. Then entrust Him with the things you're still struggling with, asking Him to give you whatever revelation you need to trust in those areas as well!

~*~ Eph 3:13 Therefore I ask you not to become discouraged about my tribulations on your behalf, since they are your glory.

Remember that Paul was a prisoner in Rome as he was writing this, and it seems that the Ephesians were struggling with discouragement. It's understandable, isn't it? Here is the man who founded the church, and then came back and spent several years building up the church and ministering and teaching... and now he is in prison. Maybe they were doing what we would be doing, praying over and over again for long years for Paul's release—a release that never came.

But Paul doesn't beg them to keep praying for his release. Instead he asks them not to be discouraged.

He also says that his tribulations are their glory. This is hard for us in America to understand, for to us, there's nothing glorious about tribulations. We consider them something to be avoided and prayed against. I think this might be something that God will have to teach many of us in the years to come.

~*~ Eph 3:14 For this reason I bend my knees before the Father, 15 from whom every family in heaven and on earth derives its name,

This is the second great prayer of Ephesians! Paul starts this one by identifying the Father as the One that our family name is derived from. What does this mean?

To me, the meaning that fits the scriptures and the context is that of God's fatherhood, since Paul adds this phrase as an extension of precisely that. The Jews and Greeks were both patriarchal societies, as ours has historical been, so the family name came from the father. This is not true of all cultures and it's shifting in our culture as well, but in the cultures that Paul was writing from and to, this was true.

The family name was the *identity* of the family. I was born identifying with the McIver family, but when I married, I transferred my identity to the Peters family.

So here, Paul is saying that all of us, when we identify God as our Father, also adopt our identity and "family name" in a spiritual sense from Him. I think the way this plays out for us is when we call ourselves "Christians," for we are calling ourselves by the name of Christ. (Yes, His name was Yeshua in Hebrew, Jesus in English, Yēsū in Chinese, Ciise in Somali, etc. But most cultures have other people with those names, while no one else that I've ever heard of was called the Christ—the Chosen One or Anointed One!)

~*~ Eph 3:16 that He would grant you, according to the riches of His glory, to be strengthened with power through His Spirit in the inner self,

His prayer for them the first time (in chapter one) was all about revelation and hope and the knowledge of everything they have and are <u>in Christ</u>, for that is what the whole first chapter was about. But chapter three is now talking about God's purpose for the church here on earth. His prayer reflects that, for he asks the Father for *power*. Paul knows that God's purposes on earth cannot be fulfilled without His power! Notice, however, that he *first* asked for revelation, and *then* he asked for power. This is the correct order. We should never ask for power without first asking for the revelation, for it is the revelation that shows us how to properly use the power. It is the revelation that protects us from using the power in the wrong way.

Also notice that he doesn't just pray, "Father, please give them power." Many people and religions seek power of many types, so Paul is specific. He is asking for their power to be received *through His Spirit in the inner self.*

Writing Prompt

What does the Holy Spirit's power on the inside of us look like? Spend a few minutes thinking about this.

_____
_____
_____
_____
_____
_____
_____
_____
_____
_____
_____
_____
_____
_____
_____
_____
_____
_____
_____
_____

Now let's consider the measure that Paul asks God to use when He strengthens them.

It's not "according to the strength they deserve."

It's not even "according to the strength they need."

He asks them to strengthen them with power "according to the riches of His glory!" Talk about undeserved grace! For this empowerment in our inner self is exactly what grace is!

~*~ Eph 3:17 so that Christ may dwell in your hearts through faith;

The words "so that" tell us that this is *why* Paul is asking God to strengthen their inner man with power.

This idea that Christ Jesus would dwell in our hearts is sometimes hard to understand, unless of course, we were raised with the idea of "asking Jesus into our heart." We've talked a lot already about the concept of us being in Christ. This is the important flip side—Jesus being in us. As we know, we can only become part of this supernatural relationship by faith. (See verse 8 of the previous chapter.)

~~~~~~~~~

John 17:22
"The glory which You have given Me I also have given to them, so that they may be one, just as We are one; 23 I in them and You in Me, that they may be perfected in unity, so that the world may know that You sent Me, and You loved them, just as You loved Me.

~~~~~~~~~

~*~ Eph 3:17 (continued) ...and that you, being rooted and grounded in love, 18 may be able to comprehend with all the saints what is the width and length and

height and depth, 19 and to know the love of Christ which surpasses knowledge, that you may be filled to all the fullness of God.

The word "and" means that this is a continuation of what Paul is praying for them to receive. These three verses are all part of this one many-layered, powerful thing—the love of God.

~~~~~~~~~~
1 John 4:8
...God is love
~~~~~~~~~~

First Paul prays that they will be *rooted and grounded* in love. This brings to mind plants and trees, for they are rooted and grounded in the soil, from which they draw sustenance. Paul is saying here that God's love isn't just something for us to *feel* or know. It's something that we can *draw our sustenance from.* God's love is an anchor for our roots to go down into. In a storm-tossed world, God's love is what we need to be grounded in, not because we "should" be grounded in it, but because love is His nature, and there is nothing more steady and sure that we can be grounded in than His very nature!

Then Paul says that he's praying that they can "comprehend... the width and length and height and depth" of God's love. His use of the word "comprehend" makes me laugh in delight. When we say that someone can't comprehend something, we're essentially saying that the subject matter is far beyond what they could actually understand. Sometimes it's said in a derogatory way, hinting that the person can't comprehend it because they're not smart enough. But here, our struggle to comprehend the love of God isn't because we're stupid. *It's because the sheer greatness of God's love is beyond human comprehension!* And yet, Paul is praying that we can comprehend it anyway, in its width and length and height and depth! He states the reality that it "surpasses knowledge," and yet his very prayer is that we *would* know it!

Paul's ending of this prayer is important. If he had left it off, then these verses would simply be about us comprehending the love of God and being rooted and grounded in it. But instead Paul says "that you may be filled to all the fullness of God." In other words, "This is why you need to be rooted and grounded in God's love and be able to comprehend this incomprehensible thing. Because this is the only way that you can be totally filled with the completeness of God." This makes sense if love is His nature!

Writing Prompt

How would you describe the love of God toward you? Write it out to God. Tell Him what you know about His love for you and ask Him to show you something new about His love for you!

_____

_____

_____

_____

_____

_____

_____

~*~ Eph 3:20 Now to Him who is able to do far more abundantly beyond all that we ask or think, according to the power that works within us, 21 to Him be the glory in the church and in Christ Jesus to all generations forever and ever. Amen

I absolutely *love* how Paul ends this prayer with a confident declaration of what God is able to do!

He doesn't say that God is just able to do what he asks. He takes it a step further and includes what we *think*, for Paul knows that sometimes we're not brave enough to ask for what we're thinking of. We "settle" even before we ask.

But actually, he doesn't just say that God can do what we're thinking of either. He takes it even further and says that God can do *beyond all* we could ask or think. In other words, even if we spend time exercising our imagination to expand what we were thinking even farther, we still wouldn't reach the limits of what God can do!

Except Paul didn't even stop there! He reached even farther to declare that God can do *abundantly* beyond all that we ask or think! And then he went even further than that to add the word "more!" *More abundantly beyond all we can ask or think!*

I love using these words in my own prayers! I have a pretty fertile imagination, so I absolutely love that God's imagination *and His ability to carry out His* plans goes far beyond my own imagination. Because let's face it... quite often my own imagination cannot think of a good way out of the situation I'm praying about. That doesn't matter at all though! Because God can do more abundantly beyond anything I can dream up!

This is why I no longer hesitate to ask God for the wildest, greatest, most life-changing things that come to mind. To me, these words are a way to say, "God this is why I'm daring to ask this— because You are able to do abundantly beyond even this! I know this prayer I'm praying doesn't even come close to the limits of what You can do, so go above and beyond, whatever that looks like."

And yet, to me, **this statement is also a confession of submission to the will of God.** For when He doesn't do the thing that I specifically asked, I can trust that He's *actually* instead doing something *beyond what I'm capable of imagining!* He's already said His plans are good and that all good things come from Him. He is the One with the true knowledge of good and evil. We *think* we know what's good and bad, but He knows what's *really* good and bad. He knew that the car accident He allowed me to go through would lead me to one of the most life-changing revelations I have ever received!

~~~~~~~~~

Jeremiah 29:11 For I know the plans that I have for you,' declares the Lord, 'plans for prosperity and not for disaster, to give you a future and a hope.

~~~~~~~~~

James 1:17 Every good and perfect gift is from above.

~~~~~~~~~

Isaiah 55:8
"For My thoughts are not your thoughts,

Nor are your ways My ways," declares the Lord.
9 "For as the heavens are higher than the earth,
So are My ways higher than your ways
And My thoughts than your thoughts."

~~~~~~~~~

Therefore, when I pray one of my outrageous prayers, and God doesn't do it, I fall back on this aspect of His nature, and I pray, "God, You didn't do that thing I wanted, but Your thoughts are higher and better than mine, and Your love is so amazing, and You do things that are beyond anything I can ask or think, so I'm going to lean on You and my knowledge of who You are instead of leaning on my own understanding. I'm trusting that whatever You're doing is *beyond* what I dreamed up, and therefore I'm okay with the fact that You didn't do what I asked. Because You are You and I trust You in Your love and Your goodness!"

All of this is what this verse means to me. All of this is why, in the last year, I've even come to a place of rest in those moments when a situation looks impossible. This rest I now have in these moments was completely unknown to me for many years! But now I think, "What does it matter if it looks impossible to me? God is able to do more abundantly beyond anything I could ask or think anyway!"

Writing Prompts

What situations are in front of you in your own life or the lives of your loved ones? Write out a prayer to God that encompasses these words as you surrender to Him the *how* and the *when* of the answer to your prayer. Let His rest encompass you as you praise Him for what He knows and what He can do!

_____

_____

Now take *this* prayer from verses 14-17 and "translate" it into a prayer for yourself.

Finally, read back through Chapter three in your own Bible, the whole way through. Which verses now leap out at you with the most meaning?

Chapter Four

Chapter three ended Paul's second prayer for the Ephesian Christians by focusing on *empowerment*. This is why he starts out chapter four with the word "therefore." Paul is essentially saying, "I have been praying that you will have the revelation of the fullness of God inside of you, because God is able to do abundantly beyond everything and anything that you could possibly dream of. **And this is why I'm praying this for you**..." This signals another shift in his letter.

To recap:

First, he wanted them to understand *who they are* <u>in Christ</u>.

Second, he wanted them to know how that changed the trajectory of their life inside Earth's timeline.

Third, he wanted them to understand *the empowerment* that comes with the fullness of God <u>in us</u>.

And now he wants to get a little more practical and talk about *what this looks like* when it is walked out inside this new reality.

Here we also see another shift in the words that Paul uses. He moves from frequently repeating how we are <u>in Christ</u> and now more frequently refers to us as His body. It means the same thing though! Every mention of His body is a reference to the reality that

Paul established so thoroughly in the first chapter, that we are <u>in Christ</u>.

~*~ Eph 4:1 Therefore I, the prisoner of the Lord, urge you to walk in a manner worthy of the calling with which you have been called,

Again Paul calls himself a prisoner of the Lord instead of a prisoner of Nero. This time he continues on to urge them about how they are living their lives. He doesn't just say, "Live and walk the right way," though. He uses the word "worthy" to indicate that this life they are called to live is a valuable one.

When Queen Elizabeth died, and the funeral arrangements went on for a week. They were worthy of a queen who had reigned over 2 billion people for 70 years.

We talk about giving God the praise that He is worthy of. Here in this verse, it is our calling that is worthy.

This contrast is remarkable. To an earthly mindset, being a prisoner is about as low as you can go as far as your station and circumstances. And yet, Paul is identifying himself as a prisoner of Jesus while he talks about the extremely high value of our calling!

Think back to chapter one when we talked about the hope of our calling, or go back to read that section again in verse 18. We talked about how knowing that we have been called is the sign or indication that we have been placed into a whole new reality by God—one where He chose us before time began and laid out a future for us that includes justifying us and glorifying us. Becoming glorified is indeed something to be worthy of!

So this little sentence shows us how Paul considered Nero's chains to be nothing, but he considered the calling that God had placed on His life—and our lives—to be everything.

This was the period of time when Nero began persecuting Christians. Paul is saying, "Look, I'm not here in chains because Nero decided to lock me up. Everything that happens to me in my life is according to the will of God because I am bound to Him. Nero doesn't have the authority over me that he thinks he has. And it is the same with you. Your calling is priceless, above and beyond everything that's happening in the empire or anything that could happen. Please remember this and live your life in a manner worthy of *this* priceless calling, instead of living as if Nero's decision to persecute Christians is what matters."

~*~ Eph 4: 2 with all humility and gentleness, with patience, bearing with one another in love,

These character attributes are all expressions of love. Remember that Paul had just prayed that they would comprehend a love (from God) that they actually could never comprehend without the revelation of the Spirit.

In 1 Corinthians 13, Paul goes into depth about what love is, including attributes not mentioned on this short list like kindness and unselfishness and rejoicing with the truth. It's interesting that the four characteristics that he chose to highlight here are all attributes that typically are needed *in dealing with difficult people.*

~~~~~~~~~
Matthew 11:29
"Take My yoke upon you and learn from Me, for I am gentle and humble in heart, and you will find rest for your souls."
~~~~~~~~~

Humility is needed when we have to deal with people who are against us. The natural human tendency is to assert our rights and declare what we know to be the truth. And yet we are <u>in Christ</u>, and He was clothed with humility, even while He was preaching truth!

~~~~~~~~~

> **Proverbs 15:1**
> A gentle answer turns away wrath,
> But a harsh word stirs up anger.

~~~~~~~~~~

Gentleness is also needed in dealing with people who are against us or whom we have a disagreement with. Jesus said He was gentle also! We therefore have abundant access to gentleness, for we are <u>in Christ</u>.

~~~~~~~~~~

> **Galatians 5:16**
> But I say, walk by the Spirit, and you will not carry out the desire of the flesh. ... 19 Now the deeds of the flesh are evident, which are: sexual immorality, impurity, indecent behavior, 20 idolatry, witchcraft, hostilities, strife, jealousy, outbursts of anger, selfish ambition, dissensions, factions, 21 envy, drunkenness, carousing, and things like these, ... 22 But **the fruit of the Spirit is love, joy, peace, patience, kindness, goodness, faithfulness, 23 gentleness, self-control;** against such things there is no law.

~~~~~~~~~~

Patience (like gentleness) is fruit of the Spirit. Paul explained in his letter to the Galatian church that the fruit of the Spirit is what our lives demonstrate when we walk by the Spirit. Sometimes we act as if the fruit of the Spirit is instead a list called "good morals you should strive to demonstrate." That's not what Paul said this list was, though!

Fruit is something that provides life and nutrition, which a healthy plant produces. Apples are the fruit of an apple tree. Strawberries are the fruit of a strawberry plant. Gentleness and patience and everything else on that list is the fruit of the Spirit. It is what *the Spirit of God* produces. **It's not what we produce!** In other words, that list is the natural result of the Spirit of God flowing through our lives.

Patience is needed as we wait on God's timing, but we all know that our primary need for patience is because we have to deal with other people!

And finally, this verse adds **"bearing with one another in love."** There are places and times where humility, gentleness, and patience are needed which *don't* involve dealing with other people, but Paul clarifies here that he is specifically referring to the need for these as we deal with people.

But which people? **One another.**

This makes me chuckle a little bit. We modern Christians read in Acts how the church was acting "with one mind."

~~~~~~~~~

Acts 2:43

Everyone kept feeling a sense of awe; and many wonders and signs were taking place through the apostles. 44 And all the believers were together and had all things in common; 45 and they would sell their property and possessions and share them with all, to the extent that anyone had need. 46 Day by day continuing with one mind in the temple, and breaking bread from house to house, they were taking their meals together with gladness and sincerity of heart, 47 praising God and having favor with all the people. And the Lord was adding to their number day by day those who were being saved.

~~~~~~~~~

I think we sometimes glorify that state of unity as if it lasted for a long time. Evidently it didn't. Because here in Ephesians, Paul is talking to the Christians of Ephesus, and if we read between the lines, we can see that he's saying, "Hey you guys! Your calling is high and priceless! Walk in a way that's worthy of it! Be humble with each other and drop your pride! Stop being harsh with each other and be gentle instead! Cut each other some slack and be patient! I'm praying that you would comprehend the incomprehensible love of God toward you because that's the only way you're going to learn how to bear with each other in a loving way! But God is able to do above and beyond all we can ask or think—including this!"

Maybe you feel that I'm reading too much into this. I know, however, that as a mother, I tend to only tell my kids what they should be doing when they're *not* doing it. Paul was their spiritual father, so to me, it's pretty clear that he saw them engaging in the opposite of these things. He saw pride and impatience and harsh dealings, so he told them to walk in humility and gentleness and patience and love.

But of course, he *only* told them this after he had reminded them of who they were <u>in Christ</u> and how he was praying that they would receive the revelation of God's amazing love for them!

~*~ Eph 4: 3 being diligent to keep the unity of the Spirit in the bond of peace.

This verse reinforces the previous verse, for Paul talks about unity and peace. His urging to "be diligent" to keep the unity indicates work. Unity and peace didn't "just happen." He knew that humility and gentleness and patience and a willingness to bear with each other were all necessary for unity and peace.

~*~ Eph 4: 4 There is one body and one Spirit, just as you also were called in one hope of your calling; 5 one Lord, one faith, one baptism,

This verse is used in many confessions of faith in many Christian denominations. For Paul, it was an extension of the last chapters when he talked about how both the Jews and the Gentiles were brought into Christ, to be one both with Christ and with each other.

This verse lists six different things that there is only one of:

One body: There weren't two bodies—a Jewish body of Christ and a Gentile body of Christ. There was just one.

One Spirit: There aren't two Holy Spirits—one of the Father and one of the Son. There is just one Spirit of both, for they are three in one. Jesus was conceived by the Holy Spirit and filled with the Holy Spirit, and He was the Word of God that existed before the dawn of time.

There is one hope of our calling, for we are all in Christ and that is where all of us—the millions of Christians who walk the earth—have been placed by God.

There is one Lord, and His name is Jesus!

There is one faith, and that is the gift of faith to simply believe that what God says is true!

Paul then says that there is one baptism.

The word "baptize" simply means "to immerse." It is always a word used to describe a physical action that symbolizes something spiritual.

The New Testament talks about John's baptism of repentance.

~~~~~~~~~~

Mark 1:4
John the Baptist appeared in the wilderness, preaching a baptism of repentance for the forgiveness of sins.

~~~~~~~~~~

John the Baptist baptized people in the Jordan river, but it was called a baptism of repentance. He immersed them in the water as a symbolic way for them to demonstrate that they were immersing themselves in repentance.

The apostles baptized people as well, but this was a symbol of belief in Jesus. Acts recounts how Paul explained this, and ironically, his explanation was being given to the Ephesian church!

Acts 19:1

Paul passed through the upper country and came to Ephesus, and found some disciples. 2 He said to them, "Did you receive the Holy Spirit when you believed?" And they said to him, "On the contrary, we have not even heard if there is a Holy Spirit." 3 And he said, "Into what then were you baptized?" And they said, "Into John's baptism." 4 Paul said, "John baptized with a baptism of repentance, telling the people to believe in Him who was coming after him, that is, in Jesus." 5 When they heard this, they were baptized in the name of the Lord Jesus. 6 And when Paul had laid hands upon them, the Holy Spirit came on them and they began speaking with tongues and prophesying.

Paul explained the *reality* behind this symbolic baptism in Romans.

Romans 6:4

Therefore we have been buried with Him through baptism into death, so that, just as Christ was raised from the dead through the glory of the Father, so we too may walk in newness of life.

In other words, this "one baptism" that Paul is referencing is *the same thing that Chapter one talked about over and over again.* Baptism means "to immerse" and we were "immersed" <u>in Christ.</u>

We were <u>in Him</u> when He died, and we were <u>in Him</u> when He rose.

And *this* is how we can walk in newness of life! This state of being <u>in Christ</u> is the only reason and the only way that we can walk "in a manner *worthy* of our calling."

~*~ Eph 4:6 one God and Father of all who is over all and <u>through all</u> and <u>in all</u>.

And there is one God.

This verse makes me smile because Paul's awe and worship of God just bursts forth again. He can't just say, "There is one God." He just *has* to follow it up with words of praise in what probably felt like a meager attempt to describe the majesty and greatness of God, for He "is over all and through all and in all."

I hope by now, you are understanding what those words mean!

I hope that the words "over all" immediately remind you of the awesome greatness and power of God!

I hope that the words "through all" remind you of how He is always present and always working through everything that goes on in your life.

I hope that the words "in all" remind you that you are <u>in Him</u> and <u>He is in you</u>!

I hope that all together, those words "over all and through all and in all" fill you with joy and the awesome security of *knowing* who your One God really is!

So Paul spends the first six verses of this chapter focusing on the necessary unity of the Church. But next he goes on to talk about the *differences* that we see in how this unity is revealed in different people.

~*~ Eph 4:7 But to each one of us grace was given according to the measure of Christ's gift.

This verse holds *so* much promise that I want to spend a little bit of time on it.

Remember that grace is God's empowerment. Paul is saying that different measures of grace/empowerment are given to each of us, since verse 10 goes on to talk about different callings. In other words, God doesn't just call someone to do something and then leave it up to them to find the way to achieve it. When He calls them, He also gives them the grace/empowerment to do it. **That's the measure He uses.**

I think two things are important to mention here.

First, this means that God does *not* measure out grace that *doesn't* match what He's called us to do. This means that we will likely see other people who have the grace to do things that we cannot do.

We should not listen when our accuser tells us that something is wrong with us because we can't do those same things! It's okay that other people have the grace to do things that we can't, for another reality is that we have been given the grace to do things that *others* can't do!

Perhaps ironically, it's always easier to see the lack in ourselves and the gifts in others.

I'm going to use an example from my own life.

When I was twenty-five years old, God supernaturally gave me the grace to play the keyboard for worship. Before that time, I could only play the piano a very, *very* little bit. Even the "intermediate" level of sheet music was very difficult for me, requiring weeks of work to figure a piece out and learn to play it. I knew the chords in my head, but when I tried to play with them, I could not figure out how to do anything more than childish repetition. Nothing flowing. Nothing beautiful. *I just couldn't figure it out,* no matter how often I tried.

But then one Sunday when our church suddenly closed and we had nowhere to go, I sat down at my piano, desperately wanting to worship… and suddenly that morning I could do what no one had taught me. I could do what I had been unable to figure out for years. I could play beautiful worship music. All I needed was the chords to guide my fingers. I've grown in that since then, and I count on that grace every Sunday.

But God did *not* give me the grace to play by ear! *I need those chords!* I *wish* I could play by ear, for it's often distracting to have to keep track of my place on the sheet in front of me. I can look away for small sections and brief moments, but even then, in my mind, I have to know the place on that sheet where I'm going to have to look in just another second or two.

Many other people can play by ear. Why can't I? It's been over 20 years since that Sunday morning, and still I cannot play a single song by ear! When it comes right down to it, I'd gladly take the ability to *memorize* the chords. But so far, I can't do that either. I'm rather rotten at rote memorization, and I have not been able to memorize the chords to any songs other than "Shout to the Lord," and I'm not sure how that one got memorized. *I haven't even been able to memorize the chords for the songs I wrote!* Not even one of them! And I have tried... oh, I have tried!

To me, this seems ridiculous. Millions of people memorize many things. I can do many things. Why can I not do this? For even a few songs?

I don't know the answer. Evidently, so far in my life, God has called me to play the keyboard for worship *with a chord book.* His grace is not there to do it without the chords. All I can do is trust that His grace will also be there to not lose or forget my chord book! I can also thank God for the grace He *did* give to me... and trust that if He ever does want me to lead worship without a chord book, then His grace will be there in a way that doesn't currently exist!

That leads me to my second point: *continuing* to rely on His grace. His grace and empowerment are a moment-by-moment thing. It's not something He hands out once and then sits back while we're expected to maintain it. It's an extension of our living, breathing relationship with Him. As such, it ebbs and flows along with His calling in our life.

I'm going to continue using my own example to demonstrate the choice that we have in these kinds of moments to walk in faith and rest in Him or not.

There have been a few times when I *did* forget my chord book at home, and I'd have to use copies from someone else's chords for the service. (This means all my notes and scribbles and so forth weren't there, so it was a lot more difficult and confusing and distracting than normal, with a lot more mistakes.) In that moment of realizing I would have to use someone else's chord sheets, I had a choice. I could panic or beat myself up for failing to remember. *Or* I could trust that God's grace would be there to cover the lack of notes. I could trust that if the music came out different because I couldn't remember what keyboard settings I normally use, or if I messed up a lot more often that Sunday, or if something else went wrong, *none of that would upset His plan for that day and what He was calling me to do that morning.*

This sometimes feels "wrong" to our self-sufficient, self-reliant, and be-responsible-for-yourself society. But God's Word says that He is strong in our weakness! Isn't accidental forgetfulness a type of weakness? Do I believe that He is able to remind me if I'm about to forget my book?

~~~~~~~~~
2 Corinthians 12:9
And He has said to me, "My grace is sufficient for you, for power is perfected in weakness.
~~~~~~~~~

In circumstances like this, we might think, "But wait a minute, it was my fault I forgot!" We might even say, "I remember thinking that I needed to grab it earlier, but I ignored it. That was probably God reminding me and I disobeyed." Well… that might be true. But the Holy Spirit is our teacher! Every teacher knows that mistakes are a part of learning. They aren't the end of the lesson—they're the middle of the lesson! Therefore we can trust God in this as well. In those moments, I pray, "Lord, I think that was Your voice. Thank You for Your patience as I learn to recognize Your voice in my spirit. I know that sometimes we learn better by mistakes than by successes, and I might have credited myself with remembering if I had listened. But it's by Your grace. Help me to listen to Your reminder next time and give You the credit for the reminder! Thank You that Your grace is going to be here this Sunday to accomplish whatever You desire, even though I'm playing off of an unfamiliar sheet."

 This type of prayer is how we chose to walk forward in faith, trusting that God is able to accomplish His desires. This is how we trust that He is greater than our mistakes, and sometimes He can use our mistakes more powerfully than He would have been able to use our perfection! What if God *wanted* the song to sound different that Sunday and chose to achieve it by using my forgetfulness as a learning moment in my journey of hearing His voice? What if someone that Sunday needed to hear and see that the keyboard player was far from perfect? What if mistake-filled worship was the type He most desired to listen to that morning? I don't know… but He does! *He always knows,* and this is what living out our faith looks like in the nitty gritty day-to-day ups and downs of life.

 We *must* drop our expectations of what *we* are supposed to achieve and measure up to. We must learn to trust that His grace *is* sufficient to accomplish what *He* desires in our lives! **That means that if the grace wasn't there, it's okay that it didn't happen.** (Whatever "it" happens to be in that moment.)

 I feel like that last statement might be shocking to some people. Our society is *full* of standards and expectations. It's instilled into us from a very early age how important it is to set goals and achieve them. We're taught that responsibility is a virtue, something is wrong if a milestone isn't achieved, and a failure to meet standards is often the justification for punishment.

 We live in a results-oriented society that worships measurements. The moment we're born, we're given APGAR scores to measure our health. When I googled those letters to make sure I remembered them right, Google's default definition was "a 1-minute score to determine how well the baby tolerated the birthing process!" Can I add some more exclamation marks to that definition? This baby isn't even an hour old, and already the baby's success in "tolerating the birthing process" is being measured, as if it's the baby's fault if he or she didn't "tolerate it" well enough!

Then our parents are told how important it is to continuously go to checkups so the doctor can measure our progress against milestones.

We start school with the expectation that we have learned certain things already or our parents have failed in preparing us. Every grade of school measures us against ever-increasing standards, and the only way to get exceptions to those standards is to get approved for another label… that is only granted if we meet a different seat of measurements.

Most jobs have performance reviews to measure our productivity and quality of work.

Even in our homes, we face the pressure to measure up to either our own or someone else's standards of what our home needs to look like. Our DIY home projects are supposed to still meet building codes. Our parenting skills are measured against other people's parenting skills and/or other people's ideas of how parenting should be done. I could go on and on.

Are all these things bad? No, of course not. Each of these standards and measurements serves a purpose, and that purpose is often good. I'm also not advocating what is often called sloppy grace—the philosophy that what we do doesn't matter. James says that faith without works is dead, which is another way of saying that the fruit of the Spirit is the fruit *of the Spirit and not the fruit of us.*

~~~~~~~~~

James 2:17
In the same way, faith also, if it has no works, is dead, being by itself.

~~~~~~~~~~

The problem that I'm addressing right now occurs when we take this results-oriented mindset and try to apply it to what the Bible calls our "walk of *faith*."

~~~~~~~~~~
2 Corinthians 5:7
For we walk by faith, not by sight.
~~~~~~~~~~

Our milestones and measurements and standards are what we *see*, and God specifically says that <u>in Him</u>, we do *not* walk according to what we see! Why? Because our sight is incomplete. That means that the standards and measures that we see and are judging ourselves against aren't accurate. God's standards and measurements are accurate, and He says in this verse of Ephesians that *His empowerment working in our life is enough to meet His standards and measurements!*

~~~~~~~~~~
1 Corinthians 13:12
For now we see in a mirror dimly, but then face to face; now I know in part, but then I will know fully, just as I also have been fully known.
~~~~~~~~~~
Isaiah 55:8
"For My thoughts are not your thoughts,
Nor are your ways My ways," declares the Lord.
9 "For as the heavens are higher than the earth,
So are My ways higher than your ways
And My thoughts than your thoughts."
~~~~~~~~~~

This is such a liberating revelation! This is how we take the pressure to measure up, and we give it to Him, and He takes the burden, and He wraps us in layers of His grace that flow moment by moment into us as He holds us and leads us.

I want to show you something.

In Matthew, Jesus was teaching his disciples, and one thing He said was this:

~~~~~~~~~~
Matthew 11:28
"Come to Me, all who are weary and burdened, and I will give you rest."
~~~~~~~~~~

David wrote this, thousands of years before:

~~~~~~~~~~
Psalm 68:19
Blessed be the Lord, who daily bears our burden,
The God who is our salvation.
~~~~~~~~~~

Remember how I shared earlier that in the Hebrew, the words "My salvation" are the word "Yeshua" which was Jesus's name in Hebrew?

You should also know that "El" is one of the Hebrew names for God. It acts sort of like a title, as it's usually paired with other words that describe God. You may have heard of names for God like "El Shaddai" (God of Heaven), "El Elyon" (God Most High), and "El Roi" (God who sees me).

If you look up Psalm 68:19 in the Hebrew (I use BlueLetterBible.org), you'll find that the second half of this verse is two words in the Hebrew: El Yeshua.

So David wrote, "Blessed be the Lord who daily bears our burden: El Yeshua." In other words, *God who is Jesus.*

And thousands of years later, Jesus gave the invitation for us to do exactly that, when He said, "Come to Me, all you who are wary and burdened, and I will give you rest."

~~~~~~~~~~
Psalm 55:22
Cast your burden upon the Lord and He will sustain you;
~~~~~~~~~~

Writing Prompt

What burdens are you bearing?

Are you struggling with expectations that you or someone else have put on you?

Are you wondering where the grace and empowerment is?

Write out these things and give them to God. Ask Him to show you what *He* desires from you. Let Him take those heavy burdens. Give Him room and time right now for Him to release you from those burdens. Ask Him to show you the grace that He's given to you and how He has measured it to be *enough for what He wants you to do!* There is such freedom in this! Open your heart to receive it!

_____

_____

_____

_____

_____

_____

~*~ Eph 4:8 Therefore it says, "When He ascended on high, He led captive the captives, And He gave gifts to people." 9 (Now this expression, "He ascended," what does it mean except that He also had descended into the lower parts of the earth? 10 He who descended is Himself also He who ascended far above all the heavens, so that He might fill all things.)

    This section is challenging for us as modern Christians to understand. I believe this is because we don't have the training in the ancient Hebrew scriptures that Paul had.

Verse 8 is a quote from Psalm 68, except Paul changed the wording slightly. The Psalm says that God received gifts, but here Paul says that He gave gifts.

~~~~~~~~~~
Psalm 68:18
You have ascended on high,
You have led captive Your captives;
You have received gifts among people,
~~~~~~~~~~

To me, if we believe that God supernaturally protected the scripture from human error, then we must simply believe that Paul's choice to do this switch was something that made sense with the knowledge of the ancient Hebrew scriptures that he had. Verse 9 also seems to state that because it says He ascended, that also means that he descended. To my own natural reasoning, it doesn't mean that at all! And yet Paul says it did.

To me, this is like if a chemist rattles something off about some elements and some chemical reaction, and he says, "Well, this chemical formula says that, so obviously it also means this." I would be thinking, "That is not *at all* obvious to me, but I'm going to trust you on it because you know so much more about this than I do." I can do the same thing here. Paul was an *expert* on the ancient Hebrew scriptures. He spent years and years and years studying everything about them. Plus, he could read them in their original language! I'm dependent on BlueLetterBible.org for any attempts I make to see what the ancient Hebrew says, but Paul knew the language, and he understood the context and subtleties and the things that were implied. So between Paul's knowledge, and God's omnipotence (being all-powerful), and God's ability to protect and preserve what He wants to preserve, I can simply trust that these verses are true.

I do find it interesting that the end of verse 9 says that Jesus had to ascend far above all the heavens *so that* He could fill all things. In other words, He could never have filled us if He had not risen victorious over everything. *Thank You, Jesus, that You did!*

~*~ Eph 4:11 And He gave some as apostles, some as prophets, some as evangelists, some as pastors and teachers,

Many Christian churches talk about "the five-fold ministry" and this is the verse that the concept comes from. Other verses in the Bible talk about other gifts and ministries and callings, so this isn't an exhaustive list of things that God calls people to do. These are five out of many things that God calls people to do. Let's go over the common/modern definition of these five words. I'm going to start with the last one because it is simplest.

Teacher

A teacher teaches things. This is quite easy for us to understand, and there is very little controversy over what it means to be called to teach. Paul is talking here not about someone who made a mental decision to become a teacher for their career. He's talking about an anointing to teach—a supernatural level of grace that enables them to teach spiritual truths and make that the focus of their life.

Some people are called to be teachers in our school education system, and some people are called to be teachers in the business world. God gives an anointing and calling for that as well! Here Paul is specifically referring to those who are called to teach Scriptural truths, as we'll see when we get to the next verse.

We have to remember, however, that almost all of us will sometimes be used by God to teach someone something. That doesn't mean our *life's calling* or focus is to *be* a teacher. We will just be called upon to teach someone something from time to time. The older we get, the more wisdom and life skills we gain, setting us up to more frequently be called upon to share what we have learned by teaching others.

Therefore, there is the action of teaching, and then there is the specific calling to teach. This chapter is talking about life callings. This will be true of the other ministry callings on this list.

Apostle

There are several different definitions that I've heard for an apostle.

One definition is that the apostles were a historical group who were personally called by Jesus in Bible times. They include "the twelve" which are named and numbered in the Bible (including Judas Iscariot who later betrayed Jesus). This definition also includes Paul as well since Paul called himself an apostle and said that Jesus appeared to him and called him. I struggle with this definition personally because Jesus called more than just "the twelve." Luke chapter ten recounts how Jesus called 70 people (or 72 depending on the translation) to go out and preach! Furthermore, this verse in Ephesians indicates that God is *still* calling people to be apostles.

Another definition I have heard is that an apostle plants churches and overseas the pastors of those churches. I've heard some denominations try to order ministry callings in ranks of authority and they usually put apostles at the top. Personally, I do not see that Paul was establishing any sort of hierarchy in this verse.

If we just go with the Greek definition of the word that Paul used in this verse, then it simply means "one who is sent out." This fits with the way Jesus sent out the 70, and how He sent out "the twelve." His final instruction (in Luke 24:49) before ascending to heaven was to wait until the Holy Spirit came upon them (which they obediently did) and then to go into all the world and teach and preach. This general definition fits with what many of us today would call a missionary.

We all know that all of us are called to "go out" and proclaim the gospel in some way, shape, or form. This was the Great Commission! Therefore, just like the ministry of teaching, some of us will be called as a missionary to "go forth," but most of us will sometimes be called for a short one-time mission to "go forth," whether it's a one-week missions trip or a "trip" across the street to our neighbor who needs us to be where they're at to minister to them.

Prophet

A prophet is someone who is specifically called to speak the words of God.

There also needs to be a distinction here between a person with an anointing to prophesy as part of their life's calling, and a time when a person—through the Holy Spirit—prophesies as an activity. In the Old Testament, King Saul was definitely not a prophet, and yet when he was first anointed to be king, the Spirit of God fell upon him, and he prophesied!

~~~~~~~~~

1 Corinthians 14:14
Pursue love, yet earnestly desire spiritual gifts, but especially that you may prophesy.

~~~~~~~~~

Paul talks in 1 Corinthians 14 about how all should desire to prophesy, which describes the activity (which any of us can do if the Holy Spirit asks it of us and gives us the words), rather than the ministry that Paul is referring to in this verse. If you noticed, a few pages back in the section for verse 4 of this chapter when I quoted from Acts 19, it says that "the Holy Spirit came on them and they began speaking with tongues *and prophesying*."

The idea of prophesying is intimidating to many of us, as it should be! To speak for God is not a thing to be taken lightly. (Although truthfully, to teach the things of God or to go out and minister to someone shouldn't be taken lightly either.)

Our Christian culture has created a "wow factor" around prophecy because we think of it as "foretelling the future." That is a limiting definition though. In the Old Testament, many prophets were primarily called by God to speak His words of rebuke against sin. Moses was called a prophet, and for him, that calling included giving the Israelites God's practical directions and leading them. Isaiah was a prophet, and the words God gave him were a huge mix of rebuke, warning, encouragement, and promises for the future.

Throughout the Old Testament, there were many false prophets and false teachers, and the New Testament has many warnings against false teachers and false prophets. Jesus even talked about people who thought they were prophesying in His name, who eventually would be turned away from Heaven with the words, "I never knew you!" (Matthew 7:21-23)

And yet, *Paul encouraged all of us to desire to prophesy.* I believe he was referring to a desire to allow the Holy Spirit to speak His words through us into other people's lives. He knows when someone needs to hear a specific scripture, or to hear that He loves them, or to hear a particular type of encouragement. When God gives us specific words to share with someone, that is the action of prophecy. The simple yet powerful words, "God loves you" are prophecy if God told you to speak them to someone!

Evangelist

The word "evangelist" means "to share good news." This is essentially the same as the apostle, except without the "going forth" part. An evangelist would be someone whose life's calling is to preach the good news right where they already are.

Again, we are all called to share the good news as an action that is part of our everyday life, even when the focus of our life's calling is something else. But some people are called to make this the focus of their life. They have a constant anointing for sharing the gospel. Billy Graham comes to mind as someone whose life calling included an anointing to preach the gospel.

Pastor

The pastoral ministry is similar to the concept of a shepherd taking care of sheep or a father taking care of spiritual children. It's an anointing and ministry that carries a day-in-and-day-out aspect of spiritual leadership and serving and caring for a local group of Christians.

Paul also uses the words elder and deacon to describe this same type of role.

~~~~~~~~~
Acts 20:28
Be on guard for yourselves and for all the flock, among which the Holy Spirit has made you overseers, to shepherd the church of God which He purchased with His own blood.
~~~~~~~~~

A pastor's calling and anointing will often include some or all of these other ministries to some extent, yet they are always a part of a personal relationship with the people whom he is called to pastor. Many pastors have to also do the teaching every Sunday, whether or not they carry the anointing for being a teacher, but they are still two different ministries.

So now that we've discussed the five ministry callings that Paul chose to highlight in this verse, let's look at what his purpose was in listing them because this isn't the end of the sentence!

~*~ **Eph 4:12 for the equipping of the saints for the work of ministry, for the building up of <u>the body of Christ</u>;**

Here's the word "for" again, telling us what God's purpose is in calling people to be apostles, prophets, evangelists, pastors, and teachers. It's <u>to equip the saints.</u>

We are those saints. In the New Testament, the word saint is frequently used to describe all those who believe. Our American culture tends to use the word "saint" to describe someone who seems to be unnaturally good, or we think of it in the Roman Catholic context.

But in the New Testament, Paul refers to all those who believe as saints.

So this verse is saying that these ministries are for equipping all those who believe. This reflects a position of servanthood and of supplying what another person needs to fulfill *their* function.

When a company gives an electrician the assignment of running electrical service to a building, they have to make sure he is fully equipped with the knowledge, the training, the equipment, the permits, the authority, the scheduling, and everything else necessary for him to complete the job.

This illustration shows how the purpose of these ministry anointings is *not* to establish a hierarchy of power and authority. It's more like servanthood! The apostle, the prophet, the evangelist, the pastor, and the teacher are all called *to make sure that everybody else in the body of Christ has what they need to fulfill their calling.*

This verse says that it's *the saints* who are doing the work of ministry. We sometimes think that the people who are part of "the five-fold ministry" are the people who are "in ministry," but this verse says that all the saints are called to do the work of ministry!

~~~~~~~~~

Mark 10:42

Calling them to Himself, Jesus said to them, "You know that those who are recognized as rulers of the Gentiles domineer over them; and their people in high position exercise authority over them. 43 But it is not this way among you; rather, whoever wants to become prominent among you shall be your servant; 44 and whoever wants to be first among you shall be slave of all. 45 For even the Son of Man did not come to be served, but to serve, and to give His life as a ransom for many."

~~~~~~~~~

What each of us does *matters*. It is vitally important! In fact, it's so extremely important that God calls specific people whose life focus and calling is to make sure that we are equipped to do what God is calling us to do!

The second half of this verse makes it even more clear. The purpose of the apostles and prophets and evangelists and pastors and teachers is *to build up the body of Christ*. This is *work*. Building.

~~~~~~~~~

1 Peter 2:5
you also, as living stones, are being built up as a spiritual house for a holy priesthood, to offer spiritual sacrifices that are acceptable to God through Jesus Christ.

~~~~~~~~~

I did not understand this when I was growing up in the church. My concept was more along the lines of how most people were "normal" while others had "high callings" and were called to lead everybody else. This is a bit backwards from what Jesus said to the disciples about them being called to serve everyone else.

Many things that Jesus taught seem backwards. The first shall be last and the last shall be first. The greatest among you is a servant. If you seek to save your life you'll lose it, but if you let it go for Him you'll find it.

Writing Prompt

Do you feel like your calling is important? How does it make you feel knowing that God has purposefully called people to spend their life making sure that you have what you need to do what He is calling you to do?

The Bible talks in a number of places about "ravenous wolves" who will try to take from the people instead of serving and equipping them.

Acts 20 tells the story of when Paul was leaving the church of Ephesus. Read what Paul says to the leaders of the Ephesian church and notice not only his warning but also his entreaties that they would serve.

~~~~~~~~~

Acts 20:29

I know that after my departure savage wolves will come in among you, not sparing the flock; 30 and from among your own selves men will arise, speaking perverse things to draw away the disciples after them. 31 Therefore, be on the alert, remembering that night and day for a period of three years I did not cease to admonish each one with tears. 32 And now I entrust you to God and to the word of His grace, which is able to build you up and to give you the inheritance among all those who are sanctified. 33 I have coveted no one's silver or gold or clothes. 34 You yourselves know that these hands served my own needs and the men who were with me. 35 In everything I showed you that by working hard in this way you must help the weak and remember the words of the Lord Jesus, that He Himself said, 'It is more blessed to give than to receive.'"

~~~~~~~~~

Do you feel like you are supported in your calling, or have you experienced people "in ministry" who seem to be in it for what they can receive from the body of Christ, rather than what they can give to the body of Christ?

It can be hard to deal with situations where those who were supposed to be servant-leaders instead only took what they could from those they were supposed to serve.

God can redeem these experiences when we give them to Him! For the blood of Jesus not only atoned for the sin that we have committed, it also atoned for the sin of others. That means that He took on Himself the weight of what others have done to us. We can surrender it and experience His redeeming power, transforming that pain into the good things that God has planned for our future!

Writing Prompt

I encourage you to spend a few minutes talking with God about any painful experiences that you may have in your past, especially if they relate to a church or person in ministry. Surrender that to God and thank Him that He is able to redeem those wrongs. He is able to bring people into your life who will indeed fulfill their calling to equip you. He will finish what He has started regardless of the wrongs that have been done!

~*~ Eph 4:13 until we all attain to the unity of the faith, and of the knowledge of the Son of God, to a mature man, to the measure of the stature which belongs to the fullness of Christ.

This is the goal that God has for these ministers who are called to equip us.

Paul talks here of unity, for God does not desire a disabled, malfunctioning, and diseased body of Christ!

He talks of the knowledge of the Son of God. Paul prayed back in the first chapter that they would receive the revelation of the knowledge of Jesus, and here he says that this is also the goal of the apostles and prophets and evangelists and pastors and teachers.

Paul talks about maturity, comparing spiritual maturity to physical/natural maturity.

And then he sums it all up, saying that the measure—the standard—is the fullness of Christ. Wow! That is God's purpose! His end goal!

This fullness refers both to the body of Christ, meaning all of us as a whole being His body here on earth, and also to the fullness of Christ dwelling in each one of us, because we are in Him, and He is in us.

~*~ Eph 4:14 As a result, we are no longer to be children, tossed here and there by waves and carried about by every wind of doctrine, by the trickery of people, by craftiness in deceitful scheming;

This verse offers a contrast to the maturity mentioned in the last verse, for it refers to spiritual children. Paul's description of spiritual children is interesting though. It serves as a stark warning, for he describes spiritual children as those who aren't established in their beliefs and are easily fooled. Paul's mention of trickery seems to be specifically talking about spiritual deception here because the trickery and scheming results in the spiritually immature being carried around "by every wind of doctrine."

The bad thing about being fooled is this: you don't know it. You think you've got it. You think you're more right than other people who disagree, and often you feel good about how you know better.

The devil knows that if he can get your pride involved, then he can use that pride to cement the false doctrine he's tricked you into believing even further into your life.

~~~~~~~~~
Proverbs 16:18
Pride goes before destruction,
And a haughty spirit before stumbling.
~~~~~~~~~

So how do we mature? How do we avoid this deception?

How can we know that at this moment, we aren't under deception of some sort or another?

Jesus gave the answer for that. He said that it's the willingness of our hearts to do the will of God—no matter what—that is necessary.

~~~~~~~~~
John 7:17
If anyone is willing to do His will, he will know about the teaching, whether it is of God, or I am speaking from Myself.
~~~~~~~~~

That doesn't seem connected to our natural mind, and yet that's what Jesus said. If we are willing to do the will of God in our everyday lives, then we will know.

Being willing to do the will of God is the tug of wills. His will versus our own. It takes humility, submission to God, and trust in

Him and His ways to truly be willing. But it's those very things—humility, submission to God, and trust in Him—that give God the permission to open our eyes so that we can see the deception that the devil is trying to snare us with. Knowing this, we can see how these next verses in Ephesians reflect this truth.

~*~ Eph 4:15 but speaking the truth in love, we are to grow up in all aspects <u>into Him who is the head</u>, that is, Christ, 16 from whom the whole body, being fitted and held together by what every joint supplies, according to the proper working of each individual part, causes the growth of the body for the building up of itself in love.

    The focus of these two verses are the two phrases that sandwich what's in the middle. Verse 15 starts with "in love" and "grow up," and verse 16 ends with "growth" and "in love" again.
    There is a connection between "growing up" spiritually and walking in love. God is love, and Jesus said that we could be identified by our love. So here we see that our spiritual maturity is all about love! As we walk in love we will mature, and as we mature, we will walk in love. Maturity and the love of God are inseparable!

~~~~~~~~~
John 15:5
"By this all people will know that you are My disciples: if you have love for one another."
~~~~~~~~~

    But look at what's in the middle of these two verses. It's another reminder of how we are in Him. Paul reminds us again, using the newer metaphor of the body, that we are in Him, and that is the only way that the growth and the love happens! For Jesus is the head, and He causes the growth! He fills us with the love.

It's all about Him!

It's about doing His will, because we are His body, and He is the head that gives out the instructions.

Again, it's not about trying to love and learning to love and going to seminars and classes. It's not about reading self-help books and reciting mantras to try to re-train ourselves into being more loving. It's also not about doing whatever this person or that person says we should do if we love them. It's about living in Him, as a part of Him, and learning to let His love flow through us and mature us.

~*~ Eph 4:17 So I say this, and affirm in the Lord, that you are to no longer walk just as the Gentiles also walk, in the futility of their minds, 18 being darkened in their understanding, excluded from the life of God because of the ignorance that is in them, because of the hardness of their heart;

Again, Paul is reminding us of what he discussed in the last chapter, about how these Gentiles in this Gentile church should no longer be walking as they used to walk, because now they are in Christ and are part of His body.

The progression of explanation that Paul offers here is important.

First, he talks about how they walk—in other words, their actions. We tend to focus on the actions as if they are what matters.

But then Paul says that they walk "in the futility of their minds," which ties their actions to what they think.

Then he says that what they think and understand is darkened due to ignorance.

Now that might seem harsh, for ignorance is sometimes not a person's fault. A person cannot know what they've never been told.

But that's not the type of ignorance that Paul is referring to, for at the end, he says that their ignorance is due to the hardness of their heart.

It's all about the heart. Again. A hardened heart is a heart that is proud and not teachable. It's a heart that cannot be convicted of sin. It's a heart that wants to go its own way rather than subject itself to the will of God.

So we see that Paul is teaching the same thing that Jesus did. Jesus said that if we are willing to do the will of the Father, as He was, then we will know the truth. God's Spirit will enable us to know what is from Him and what is deception. And Paul said that those who *aren't* willing and have hardened their hearts remain in ignorance and darkness. How they walk will reflect that.

So we see that the *willingness* to do whatever God asks is absolutely crucial to the avoidance of deception!

Writing Prompt

I encourage you to spend some time searching your heart and digging to the bottom of your willingness to do *anything* that God asks of you. Once you've found the bottom, give it all to God. Ask Him to show you more of His goodness and His love for you, for that is the secret to increasing our willingness!

_____

_____

_____

_____

_____

_____

_____

~*~ Eph 4:19 and they, having become callous, have given themselves up to indecent behavior for the practice of every kind of impurity with greediness.

The word 'callous' is another reference to the hardness of heart.

Indecent behavior might be defined differently depending on your culture, your beliefs, and many other factors. No matter what we would list under indecent, it's very likely that the list is almost entirely things that *we* don't do, but *other* people do.

But then Paul adds greediness. I don't know about you, but greediness is a little harder to consider myself to be innocent of. Greediness is one of Love's opposites though, so this is a reminder of something that will naturally disappear as we walk more and more in the love of God. I want that!

~*~ Eph 4:20 But you did not learn Christ in this way, 21 if indeed you have heard Him and have been taught <u>in Him</u>, just as truth is <u>in Jesus</u>, 22 that, in reference to your former way of life, you are to rid yourselves of the old self, which is being corrupted in accordance with the lusts of deceit, 23 and that you are to be renewed in the spirit of your minds, 24 and to put on the new self, which in the likeness of God has been created in righteousness and holiness of the truth.

Paul has talked about sin quite a few times, but in this instance, he talks about taking off the old self and putting on the new self as if they are clothing. This metaphor is used a number of times in both the Old Testament and the New Testament, with dirty garments symbolizing a sinful old self. In each instance, the new garments are created by God and are garments of righteousness.

There's a direction here between the ones about taking off the old self and putting on the new self. We must also "be renewed in the spirit of our mind." Isn't it interesting that this renewing happens in the transition between the old self and the new self? This is important, for without the renewing, we might be tempted to think that this change of self is just a costume on the outside to make us look different. But that is clearly *not* the metaphor that the Bible means when it refers to robes of righteousness, because renewing of the mind is a change *in who we are.*

Notice again that it doesn't say "renew your mind" as if it's something we can do ourselves. No, it says, "Be renewed" which is passive. God is the one who renews us; we simply present ourselves to Him in submission, surrendering our lives to Him so that He can do this renewing work. **That is how we rid ourselves of the old self and put on the new self.**

Are you ready for another slight shift? This shift doesn't line up with the end of a chapter, but Paul didn't decide the chapter lengths anyway. Church fathers many years later did so that people like us could more easily reference portions of the letter.

The shift that happens right here gets even more practical. The rest of this chapter, all of chapter five, and part of chapter six look *very* practical, for they focus on actions that we can see. These verses can easily be taken to look like a new set of laws. "Do this; do that. Don't do this, and don't do that." Many of them have been used that way in the church.

But remember the context! Paul did *not* start the letter off with these. This *isn't* a list of laws to follow in order to be righteous. Paul spent a *very* long time explaining to us just who we are in Christ, how we are empowered, and all that it means. These things that we're going to start talking about are a description of the new self that God created for us. **God created it.** *We* cannot create it!

Remember this as you continue reading. We do not want to fall into the same trap that the Galatian church fell into, accepting salvation by faith but then acting like everything after that moment was up to them and their own efforts.

~~~~~~~~~~

Galatians 3:1

You foolish Galatians, who has bewitched you, before whose eyes Jesus Christ was publicly portrayed as crucified? 2 This is the only thing I want to find out from you: did you receive the Spirit by works of the Law, or by hearing with faith? 3 Are you so foolish? Having begun by the Spirit, are you now being perfected by the flesh?

~~~~~~~~~~

Also notice how many of these things that Paul is about to talk about are actually principles rather than rules.

~*~ Eph 4:25 Therefore, ridding yourselves of falsehood, speak truth each one of you with his neighbor, because we are parts of one another.

Here Paul is telling us that lies are not a part of the new self that God created. I love how he explains *why* they aren't! "Because we are parts of one another." He is referencing the fact that we are all one body (from verse 4) as the reason why lying cannot be a part of the new self that is in Him. It would be as if our left hand was lying to our right hand about what it was doing! In fact, that's a phrase we like to use to describe disfunction in a business or group of people, isn't it? We say that the left hand doesn't know what the right hand is doing. This type of disfunction shouldn't exist in the body of Christ either! Therefore, we must speak truth to each other. This is a principle that fits with the unity that God has called us to.

Speaking truth to one another also includes vulnerability and honesty in who we are, how we're doing, and what we're struggling with. Social media apps all offer filters to make our selfie pictures look better, and all too often, we put the same sort of filters on our very selves when we walk into church. The various members of the body are supposed to minister to each other, but how can we do this if we hide when we need ministry? The parts of our own physical bodies minister to each other. If one arm needs scratching, the other happily offers the scratch. If a part of our body is sore or injured, other parts of our body compensate. This would not be possible if our body parts did not communicate needs to the other parts.

We need to learn to speak (and graciously receive) this kind of truth from each other as well, so we can pray for and encourage each other. How many times, when we're asking God for a word about something, is He wanting to give that word to someone else so that they can (through prophecy) pass that message to us? This is how our body functions, and this is how God desires His body to function as well.

~*~ **Eph 4:26 Be angry, and yet do not sin; do not let the sun go down on your anger, 27 and do not give the devil an opportunity.**

Anger is a natural emotion that even Jesus experienced, so here Paul provides a warning. He doesn't say not to get angry. He warns that it can lead to sin and give the devil an opportunity if we allow ourselves to remain angry. Thus, the new self learns to handle anger, rather than letting anger control it. Again, this is a principle of who we are submitting ourselves to. Are we submitting to God's Spirit so that His fruit can flow, or are we submitting to the devil and the flesh (which likes to get angry)?

~*~ **Eph 4:28 The one who steals must no longer steal; but rather he must labor, producing with his own hands what is good, so that he will have something to share with the one who has need.**

This verse brings the principle of a good work ethic together with the principle of generosity. American society teaches that the whole reason for working hard is to get ahead, but here Paul explains that the new self works hard so that it can be generous! Why? Because God is a generous God and His Spirit living in us will also be generous!

~*~ **Eph 4:29 Let no unwholesome word come out of your mouth, but if there is any good word for edification according to the need of the moment, say that, so that it will give grace to those who hear.**

This verse is about our speech, but Paul doesn't tell us to avoid lists of forbidden curse words. Instead, he says that the new self's words demonstrate a principle that focuses on the wholesomeness of the words being used, as well as the intent behind them. The new self is not concerned with rules of what to say and not say. The new self is concerned with how the person listening will receive it. The new self—guided by the Spirit of God—wants to edify and give grace and empower those who hear. The Spirit of God knows what each person around us needs, so He will lead us in this way, as we learn to walk in this new self!

~*~ Eph 4:30 Do not grieve the Holy Spirit of God, by whom you were sealed for the day of redemption.

Are you familiar with what it means when we say that someone "brought grief to his mother"? This is what this verse is referring to, except instead of our mother, it's the Holy Spirit who dwells inside of us.

Because the Holy Spirit fills us (if indeed we are Christians), then what we look at, He is forced to look at. What we do, He participates in. What we don't do, He has also not done. So when we willingly indulge in sin—or even indulge in worthless things—we are forcing Him to participate as well. So if it's something that He has no desire to participate in, then we grieve Him.

The closer we get to God, the more sensitive we get to the feelings of the Holy Spirit. We might discover that something that once didn't bother our conscience at all now grieves Him. This can sometimes be challenging when others around us (even other Christians) are doing the thing with no qualms of conscience at all! It takes sensitivity and humility to step back and away from the thing that is grieving Him while not judging those who are still happily engaging in whatever-it-is. Sometimes we can experience persecution (hopefully mild, but often still uncomfortable) in these situations, but the Holy Spirit is with us to lead us and comfort us!

~*~ Eph 4:31 All bitterness, wrath, anger, clamor, and slander must be removed from you, along with all malice.

This verse has quite a list, doesn't it? Paul is still focusing on how the new self walks in unity with others as the body of Christ, so he's listing things that cause issues in our relationships with others.

It's interesting that some of the things on this list aren't always a sin, so let's look at them.

Bitterness is often used to describe the feelings that we hold onto when someone wrongs us. It's natural to be hurt, but when we *hold onto* our indignation and refuse to forgive, it actually becomes hate. That's what the Hebrew word here is describing.

Wrath is extreme anger and indignation. God is described several times as being wrathful, so it's not always a sin!

Anger is mentioned again, and we know God gets angry about things!

Clamor refers to a Hebrew word that describes a loud outcry. There are certainly times when an outcry is a natural response!

Slander is speaking negative things against someone. It's interesting to notice that it's not confined to those who are innocent. In other words, when someone who holds different religious, political, or cultural opinions than us does something that we think is terrible, and we pass the news on about how awful the things they are doing is, that's slander too!

And finally malice is listed, which is a desire to injure someone.

So if this list isn't a clear list of things that are always sin, then why does Paul list them here? I think the answer is in remembering the context here. He's been talking about unity in the body of Christ. All of these things, if allowed to remain in our relationships, will indeed create division in the body of Christ. That is why he says to "remove" them from us. When we discover that they are active, we need to get rid of it, because if we hold onto it, we will contribute to divisions.

~*~ **Eph 4:32 Be kind to one another, compassionate, forgiving each other, just as God <u>in Christ</u> also has forgiven you.**

This verse is the flip side of the last one. This is what the Spirit, alive in your new life, is going to look like as He moves in your relationships with those around you.

Instead of being bitter and angry and wrathful, we choose to forgive. Instead of slandering we are compassionate and kind. This promotes unity.

Now that we've gone through these verses, think of your own life. What opportunities do you have each week to make a choice between actions that increase division or promote unity? Maybe it's school. Maybe it's church. Maybe it's social media and what you post or "like" there. Maybe it's only in your thoughts, for bitterness inside your heart can cause you to pull back from those that God is calling you to work with.

Writing Prompt

Talk with God about these things, but remember that these things are *not* a result of how successful you are at trying harder. They are either the fruit of the Spirit or the fruit of the fleshly part of you.

Allow the Holy Spirit to convict you and inspire you, and respond by asking Him to show you how to surrender those parts of you that you have been holding back, for *that* is what will allow His Spirit to reign even more in your life. Then *you* will be walking in unity with Him and with others who are walking with Him!

_____

_____

_____

Chapter Five

Chapter five is a very practical chapter which continues the examples of what the new life looks like and what God is leading us all toward.

This move from the "spiritual and unseen" to the "natural and seen" has several important aspects to it.

As we talked about already, Jesus said that this is how things flow. What is seen in the natural is a result of what exists inside of us spiritually. Therefore it makes sense that Paul talked about the spiritual realities that we have become a part of before he moved on to what it looks like in the natural.

It can be tempting then to wonder *why* Paul gave directions for how to walk this out. If what we do and how we act and what we say is a result of what is inside of us, then why would we need to be told to "do" this or that?

The answer, as Paul explained in Romans chapter seven, is that there is a war inside of us between the spirit and the flesh. We sometimes need help identifying which is which inside of ourselves. That's why it's so helpful to have Paul's instructions like those in this chapter, Jesus's Sermon on the Mount (in Matthew 5-7), and

Romans 12. We are in a training process as we learn which influences and impulses and thoughts and desires are from Jesus living inside of us and which are from our flesh.

Sometimes it's easy to determine. When the impulse and desire is to reach out and comfort someone who has wronged us previously, we know that this is from the Spirit of God inside of us, because this is love! When the impulse is to lie in order to save some money or get the better of someone, it's easy to know that this impulse is from the flesh.

But what about the many "iffy" situations in our day-to-day lives? What about those moments when we are confronted with a situation, and we recognize conflicting desires and feelings within us, and we honestly aren't sure which are from God's Spirit, and which are from the flesh?

This is why the Bible gives the practical instructions. These are our "signposts" to help us know.

Here's an example: The last chapter talked about slander. Let's say we're in a group of people who are talking about all the wrongs done by the opposing political party, and we're wondering if it's okay to join in the conversation. After all, they say they are listing all the bad things the opponent has done because it's "important to know" for voting purposes. So we whisper a quiet prayer for direction from God. His Spirit reminds us of Paul's instruction to avoid slander. Suddenly we know that the desire to share the latest things we heard that so-and-so has done is from the flesh, and that little nudge to abstain is from the Spirit of God.

That is what the instructions in this chapter are for—to help us identify the quiet nudges from God's Spirit. They're often *much* more gentle than the loud desires of our flesh!

So let's look at what Paul says.

~*~ Eph 5:1 Therefore be imitators of God, as beloved children;

Wow. Be imitators of God! That could be intimidating if we hadn't already learned that we are <u>in Christ</u> already, and the Spirit of God is our spiritual, life-giving breath!

I love that we are reminded that we are His beloved children.

~~~~~~~~~~
John 3:1
See how great a love the Father has given us, that we would be called children of God; and in fact we are.
~~~~~~~~~~

God wants us to know that the instructions He's about to give us (through Paul) are not the demands of a harsh dictator who enjoys creating hard rules "just because." No! He is only asking us to follow in His footsteps and imitate Him, and we are His children. As Jesus is "the Son of God," so we also are sons and daughters of God, since we are <u>in Christ</u>. Therefore we are being asked to walk out our life here on earth as beloved children who are simply following in His footsteps.

~*~ Eph 5:2 and walk in love, just as Christ also loved you and gave Himself up for us, an offering and a sacrifice to God as a fragrant aroma.

Paul says that our walk should be "in love," and he gave us Jesus's example.

Jesus said all of the law is summed up in His commandment to love God and love other people.

~~~~~~~~~~
Matthew 22:36
"Teacher, which is the great commandment in the Law?" 37 And He said to him, "'You shall love the Lord your God with all your heart, and with all your soul, and with all your

mind.' 38 This is the great and foremost commandment. 39 The second is like it, 'You shall love your neighbor as yourself.' 40 Upon these two commandments hang the whole Law and the Prophets."

~~~~~~~~~~

Everything is to be done in love.
But again, this is the love that is now <u>in us</u> because we are <u>in Christ</u>, for He gave Himself completely on our behalf!

~*~ Eph 5:3 But sexual immorality or any impurity or greed must not even be mentioned among you, as is proper among saints; 4 and there must be no filthiness or foolish talk, or vulgar joking, which are not fitting, but rather giving of thanks. 5 For this you know with certainty, that no sexually immoral or impure or greedy person, which amounts to an idolater, has an inheritance in the kingdom of Christ and God.

These three verses appear to list a variety of things, but they actually all fit together.
Note that verse 3 lists three things: sexual immorality, impurity, and greed. Then verse 5 comes back to those three things. So let's talk about them.
Sexual immorality probably doesn't need much explanation, for there is a lot of talk in Christian circles in recent years about various types of sexual immorality and how prevalent it is becoming in our twenty-first century world. In fact, it might be getting close to what it was in the Roman society that the church of Ephesus was founded in the middle of!
Ephesus was one of the largest cities in the Roman empire, and the Temple of Artemis was a *huge* attraction as one of the Seven

Wonders of the Ancient World. Acts 19 mentions this temple, and I encourage you to read that chapter to gain a bit of reference as you read through this chapter.

There's a lot of controversy regarding exactly what the Ephesian version of Artemis represented, but we do know that Roman and Greek culture of the time involved a lot of sexual immorality. Many things were not considered immoral at the time, except by Christians. In fact, it was because of Christians that Roman society began changing. Within a few hundred years of Paul's time, Christianity was the official religion of the Roman empire. Most sexual immorality was outlawed in the Roman Empire, stayed forbidden through the Dark Ages in Europe, continued to be condemned through the Reformation and the Age of Enlightenment, and remained forbidden (socially if not legally) in Europe and the New World over most of the past six hundred years.

Thus, our current culture's "new" views on sexuality are less something new and more like the world returning to the state the Roman Empire was in when God sent Jesus into it to begin with.

Impurity is the second thing Paul listed here, and perhaps your first thought is that it is related to sexual immorality. There certainly is some overlap, but there are many other parts of life that should involve purity.

Consider purity of motives and desires. We might have a desire to accomplish something and tell others that we want to do this thing to help other people. We might even tell ourselves that's why we want to do it. However, if we consider the purity of our motives, we might discover less glorious motives mixed up in our heart such as self-glory, competitiveness, to make someone like us more, or to prove someone else wrong.

Then there is impurity of speech which verse 4 talks about. Paul says to avoid "foolish talk," and I wonder if some aspects of our modern sense of humor might grieve God's Spirit. I love that Paul offers an alternative for our speech patterns—though giving of thanks! I wonder how much our society would change if even 25% of the average conversation or news article or social media post became some type of thanksgiving: either testifying of what God has done, thanking Him that His grace and provision will be sufficient for the situation under discussion, thanking the person we're talking to, telling others how thankful we are for those who are being gossiped about, etc.

Greed is the third item that Paul lists twice. Selfishness and covetousness are the words used in some translations, for these mean the same thing. These synonyms help us to realize that greed is about more than just money and possessions, for we can also be greedy for recognition, power, or even just greedy for our own way!

It's interesting that in verse 5, Paul says that greed is idolatry! He repeats this in his letter to the Colossian church as well.

~~~~~~~~~

Colossians 3:5
Therefore, treat the parts of your earthly body as dead to sexual immorality, impurity, passion, evil desire, and greed, which amounts to idolatry.

~~~~~~~~~

How is this so?
The answer is because greed/covetousness/selfishness is essentially worship of ourselves. It's a statement to God that what He has provided for us is not enough. We think we know better than He does, and we think that we ought to have more! Wow.

So verse 3 in this chapter says that these things "must not even be mentioned" among us! That is really raising the bar, similar to how Jesus raised the bar when He talked about how harboring hate in our hearts was the same as murder.

Then verse 5 says that those who practice these things "have no inheritance in the kingdom of Christ and God."
Let's think about what that actually means.

I have heard some teachings that this phrase means that people who practice sexual immorality can't be saved and won't go to heaven. Interestingly I have *never* heard a Christian claim that a greedy person can't be saved and won't go to heaven, even though sexual immorality and greed carry the same consequence in this verse of Ephesians!

So let's consider a few related principles as we think about what "no inheritance" means.

First is the question of whether we are saved. Does it happen the moment we accept Jesus Christ as our Savior and make Him the Lord of our life? Or are we only saved once we have had our lives completely transformed in practice and gone through many levels of grace and learned to walk in freedom from everything we were a slave to before we made Jesus our Lord?

Most if not all of us would easily agree that we are saved the moment we accept Jesus Christ as our Savior.

So is Paul saying that these three types of sin are "special"? Is he saying that if you die before they are completely gone from your life, then you aren't going to Heaven after all?

I think most Christians agree that getting rid of the sin in our life is a process that *starts* when we make Jesus our Lord and continues throughout our life. If we still struggle with selfishness (which I still struggle with), it's proof that God isn't done working yet. It's *not* proof that I'm not saved.

Put that way, I think it's clear that Paul's reference to our "inheritance in the kingdom" is *not* a reference to Heaven.

~~~~~~~~~~

Mark 1:14
Jesus came into Galilee, preaching the gospel of God, 15 and saying, "The time is fulfilled, and the kingdom of God is at hand; repent and believe in the gospel."

~~~~~~~~~~

Jesus also talked over and over again about the Kingdom of God (or the Kingdom of Heaven depending on which of the gospels you're reading). He said it was "at hand" because He had arrived to bring it to earth. Many of His parables are about the Kingdom of God and this new reality that we can be a part of because we are <u>in Him</u>! If you want to look at them, just type in "kingdom of God" or "kingdom of Heaven" into BibleGateway.com, and you'll be amazed at all the verses that come up!

In Romans, Paul defines the Kingdom of God this way:

~~~~~~~~~
Romans 14:17
For the kingdom of God is not eating and drinking, but righteousness and peace and joy in the Holy Spirit.
~~~~~~~~~

In this verse from Romans, it is clear that Paul is talking about the contrast between the spiritual life that Jesus brought to earth and the physical things of life which we can touch and taste and feel. Since Paul actually explained in Romans what he meant when he talked about the kingdom of God, I think we need to use his definition when we read this verse in Ephesians.

~~~~~~~~~
John 17:15
I am not asking You to take them out of the world, but to keep them away from the evil one. 16 They are not of the world, just as I am not of the world.
~~~~~~~~~
Romans 8:16
The Spirit Himself testifies with our spirit that we are children of God, 17 and if children, heirs also, heirs of God

and fellow heirs with Christ, if indeed we suffer with Him so that we may also be glorified with Him.

~~~~~~~~~

Furthermore, we also know that we are now "in the world" but no longer "of the world." Spiritually, we have been transferred to the kingdom of God because we are in Christ!

So if we take this definition and we insert it into verse 5, here's what it says: "For this you know with certainty, that no sexually immoral or impure or greedy person, which amounts to an idolater, has an inheritance in righteousness and peace and joy in the Holy Spirit." Wow.

Notice that he *doesn't* say, "Any person who is seeking God and occasionally slips up in these sins but is quick to repent and continue pursuing a relationship with God." This is a good thing, especially since Jesus said that we can harbor sin in our heart, even if we don't follow through on the actions!

No. He lists three things we won't inherit: **righteousness**, **peace**, and **joy**. He is saying that when these sins are in our life so much that these adjectives describe us, *we're not inheriting Jesus' righteousness* (which is faith according to Romans. Remember our discussion about Ephesians 2:15?) Thus, *a person embracing these sins is going to struggle to believe what God says about them!*

~~~~~~~~~
Romans 4:5
But to the one who ...believes in Him who justifies the ungodly, his faith is credited as righteousness.
~~~~~~~~~

Paul is saying that when these sins are in our life, we're *not able to inherit* **peace** *and* **joy**. Thus, *a person who embraces these sins is going to be filled with turmoil and perhaps depression*, for these things rush in to attack us when we do not have the peace of God guarding our hearts and the joy of the Lord strengthening and protecting us!

~~~~~~~~~
Nehemiah 8:10
"Do not be grieved, for the joy of the Lord is your refuge."
~~~~~~~~~
Philippians 4:7 And the peace of God, which surpasses all comprehension, will guard your hearts and minds in Christ Jesus.
~~~~~~~~~

Faith, peace, and joy are part of the inheritance that Paul prayed in Ephesians chapter one that they would have. Here, he is warning that if we choose to embrace these sins, we're giving up part of our inheritance in Christ Jesus. We're essentially choosing the sin over the inheritance.

~*~ Eph 5:6 See that no one deceives you with empty words, for because of these things the wrath of God comes upon the sons of disobedience. 7 Therefore do not become partners with them;

This warning is against falling prey to "empty words" that flatter our mind and ego and emotions. We like to talk about politicians who use empty words to get elected, and then once they gain office, they don't (or are unable to) follow through on what they promised.

Religious leaders and salesmen and motivational speakers and plenty of others also sometimes use empty words to deceive us!

Those are commonly considered examples of empty words, but we will also encounter empty words *much* more often in our everyday lives.

Verse 7 uses the word "partner" to highlight the fact that when we fall for empty words, we are in essence joining ourselves to them. We are aligning part of our life with whatever they're "selling."

If we jump to verse 6, Paul talks about how this invites the wrath of God. Ouch! If we become partners with them when we fall for it, then it's not only they who are under this wrath due to disobedience—it's us too!

This is a strong warning to examine closely *anything* which appeals to fleshly desires.

What fleshly desires are often appealed to today?

- The desire for affirmation can suck me into believing any lie that matches what I *want* to be true, and the desire to prove I'm right can entice me to pass that lie on to others!
- The desire for having my own way can suck me into agreeing with anyone who offers me a chance to have it. If I actually do get my own way, I'm enticed to walk in greed and selfishness!
- The desire for love can suck me into believing that someone really cares about me when they really just want something from me, which can then entice me into compromising my standards to try to keep the love that I never really had to begin with.

Writing Prompt

What do you feel are the most dangerous empty words in your world? Talk with God about them, and then ask Him to open your ears to hear His words. Give Him permission to show you if you are currently believing empty words in any area of your life!

_____

_____

_____

_____

_____

~*~ Eph 5:8 for you were once darkness, but now you are light in the Lord; walk as children of light 9 (for the fruit of the light consists in all goodness, righteousness, and truth), 10 as you try to learn what is pleasing to the Lord.

Paul is again using the metaphor of darkness and light to refer to our spiritual vision and understanding, just as he did in chapter one when he prayed that the eyes of our heart would be enlightened. Here, he says that we *were* darkness but are now light. This fits with Jesus's statement that we are the light of the world.

> Matthew 5:14
> "You are the light of the world. A city set on a hill cannot be hidden."

But darkness and light aren't just states that exist. Light is productive and darkness is not. Just as the sunlight is used by plants for photosynthesis and produces warmth which then generates wind and works with the rotation of the earth to produce ocean currents, so spiritual light produces things. Paul could have probably listed many things that it produces, but he chose to list "all goodness" which is pretty encompassing! This describes our actions—the fruit of the Spirit.

Then he adds righteousness, which we must again remember comes through faith. This makes sense, for it is the spiritual light coming from God that enables us to see and understand and therefore believe what God says, which is "credited to us as righteousness."

> Romans 4:5
> But to the one who does not work, but believes in Him who justifies the ungodly, his faith is credited as righteousness.

Then Paul adds truth as the fruit of the light. Truth is how things *really* are, so it is clear that light is necessary to see how things really are.

Verse 10 is a continuation of the part of the sentence that began in verse 8. "Walk as children of light... *as you try to learn what is pleasing to the Lord.*" This is, of course, the reason for this chapter—to assist us in learning to identify which impulses and desires are from the flesh and which are from the Spirit of God dwelling inside of us.

~*~ Eph 5:11 Do not participate in the useless deeds of darkness, but instead even expose them; 12 for it is disgraceful even to speak of the things which are done by them in secret. 13 But all things become visible when they are exposed by the light, for everything that becomes visible is light.

 I think it is interesting that verse 11 talks about the "useless" deeds of darkness instead of the "evil" deeds of darkness. There are indeed evil deeds done in darkness, but it seems that in this moment, Paul desires to focus on those that are useless. We might not describe them as evil, but they're still useless!

 The second half of verse 11 appears to contradict verse 12 at first. Verse 11 says to expose the deeds of darkness, which our natural mind might think means that we have to talk about it. After all, that's how things are exposed in our natural world. Consider an exposé done by the media, or an investigation done by the government, or the report provided by a whistleblower. There is absolutely no way that any of these things can expose something without talking about it. And yet here, Paul says that it's disgraceful for us to even speak of these deeds of darkness!

 The answer to this apparent contradiction is in verse 13. Paul points out that these deeds of darkness "will become visible" when they are *exposed* to light. This fact is so obvious to us in the natural that we don't think twice about reaching for the light switch when we enter a room and need to see what exists in the previously-dark room. But what does this mean spiritually?

 Well, Jesus said that we *are* the light of the world. Our very presence in a situation will cause the deeds of darkness to become visible. It might not be immediate, but it happens!

 This is why God sends His people into dark situations. This is why He doesn't give us lives where everything is perfect and nothing bad ever happens and no one ever does anything against us. Such a paradise-like existence is waiting for us in heaven, but here on earth, there are billions of dark situations, and *He needs His people to carry His light into them!*

It's easy to consider a missionary as going into a dark place to spread the gospel, but what about the dark situations that exist in our own communities? Have you ever walked into a new job that looked promising or a project where they asked for your help… and then when you got into the middle of it, it seemed like everything fell apart because this person wasn't doing their job and that person was engaged in underhanded tactics? Perhaps you lamented, "God, am I really supposed to be here? What is going on? This situation is a mess!"

Maybe this is what it looks like to have the light walk into a dark situation, and all of the useless deeds become visible.

Maybe this is *why* God asked you to go there. Because that situation needed His light!

This is also why we need to learn to recognize God's leading with certainty, because walking into a dark situation is not something to be done casually! But when God says, "Go!" we can walk confidently, knowing that we *are* the light, and because we are in Christ, the darkness has no power to touch us as long as we are resting in Him!

Writing Prompt

What dark situations are closest to you and impact your life? I encourage you to have a conversation with God about them.

_____

_____

_____

_____

~*~ Eph 5:14 For this reason it says,
"Awake, sleeper,
And arise from the dead,
and Christ will shine on you." ~

    This is another of those places where Paul *sort of* quotes from the Old Testament. The closest Old Testament scripture (at least if we're searching English translations) is Isaiah 60 which has the same themes as these verses. It's one of my favorite passages, for God is describing—many years before Jesus called us the light—how God's intent was always for His people to be the light in the darkness. Furthermore, these verses in Isaiah say that the light of God shining on us *will draw others*.

~~~~~~~~~~

Isaiah 60:1
"Arise, shine; for your light has come,
And the glory of the Lord has risen upon you.
2 For behold, darkness will cover the earth
And deep darkness the peoples;
But the Lord will rise upon you
And His glory will appear upon you.
3 Nations will come to your light,
And kings to the brightness of your rising.

~~~~~~~~~~

~*~ Eph 5:15 So then, be careful how you walk, not as unwise people but as wise, 16 making the most of your time, because the days are evil.

    Paul was saying 2,000 years ago that the days were evil! Remember that the state of the world now is only getting close to the ungodliness that existed in Paul's days. A good part of our entertainment includes Hollywood-created murder and violence, but is that better or worse than the gladiator arenas of Paul's day? Homosexuality today is becoming an accepted part of society, and it was in Paul's day too. (At least, it was acceptable if you were a man and were wealthy enough to own slaves to use for this purpose.) Sex with anyone is prevalent today, just as it was in Paul's day. Marriage back then was merely a legal or financial contract; nobody expected you to actually love or be faithful to your husband or wife. (We might still be a little better in that regard today, for adultery is still frowned upon by most of today's society.)

So Paul wasn't kidding when he said that the days are evil. But what did he say we should do because of this? *Walk wisely.* Don't just fumble along doing whatever seems right in the moment, but recognize that what you do and say *matters*. It might have long-lasting implications.

Don't hide; *walk*.

He also said to *make the most of your time.* This fits in with his earlier calls to avoid empty words. It also fits in with his statement that the deeds of darkness are *useless.* I think sometimes we think that what we do matters only as far as making sure that we don't do things that are wrong. Our society tends to think that "if it's not hurting anyone, it's okay." Even we Christians act as if this is true if we look at how we spend our time. And yet Paul says to "make the most of your time!"

What does that mean practically?

Does it mean that we need to be working or ministering all the time? Definitely not, for God issued *commands* that His people rest. But how many of the non-working things that we do *really* qualify as rest? If we're spending hours on social media, is that really bringing us rest or is it just riling us up? What kind of rest fits in with Paul's instruction to make the most of our time?

God also issued commands that His people regularly stop working to celebrate and feast! (In fact, He gave the Jews *lots* of holidays!) But giving thanks and remembering the things that He had done for them were intended to be a big part of those holidays!

We do this as part of our Easter and Thanksgiving and Christmas holidays, but what about when we go on vacation? Do we leave our Bible at home, or do we make thanking and praising God and remembering what He has done part of those holidays also? (I like the way the Europeans call any vacation "going on holiday.") We can therefore assume that, in God's eyes, taking holidays to rejoice and rest and celebrate His goodness with our loved ones is also part of His plan for us to make the most of our time!

What about the work that we do? In Colossians, Paul explained how to make the most of our time in our jobs, giving it our best effort and knowing that we are really serving God in our jobs (since it is where He has currently placed us) rather than serving our bosses. Even if our boss *thinks* we're there for their benefit, we know better!

~~~~~~~~~

Colossians 3:23

Whatever you do, do your work heartily, as for the Lord and not for people, 24 knowing that it is from the Lord that you will receive the reward of the inheritance. It is the Lord Christ whom you serve.

~~~~~~~~~

As Ephesians continues, Paul will offer more tips on how to make the most of our time as we fellowship with other Christians and in our families.

Think about how you spend your time, but don't apply human standards to it. I even encourage you to think twice about applying church standards to how you spend your time, for many old church principles focused on sacrifice and service but ignored rest and individual obedience to God. Instead, have a conversation with God about how you spend your time.

~~~~~~~~~

1 Samuel 15:22

"Behold, to obey is better than a sacrifice,"
~~~~~~~~~

    Which parts of your days are spent doing things that He has called you to do? Let Him speak to you and encourage you in how you can do those things joyfully for Him, drawing upon His grace and strength, instead of working in weariness and obligation.

    Which parts of your days does He desire you to adjust? Perhaps He's been whispering for a while that there is something that He wants you to lay down, or perhaps a season is ending and what He called you to do last month is just about over. He might be asking you to lay down something that you enjoy, but He also might be asking you to surrender something that you can't stand and don't know how to get rid of! Ask for His leading, peace, and grace/empowerment to change course.

    Are you getting enough rest, and are you involving Him in your rest times? This doesn't mean that you only rest in your prayer closet. (Though sometimes we might indeed fall asleep there! But what better place is there to rest?)

    Rest times with family might mean asking God to give you the words of encouragement that each family member needs as you listen to their stories and struggles. Rest times visiting another location might include God opening your eyes to something amazing that He wants to show you there. Rest times at an amusement park might include praising Him for the chance to have fun and laugh with friends, keeping your conversation godly and encouraging, and being kind to any grumpy people you come in contact with. He wants to be *involved* in your life—even your times of rest and celebration and fun and rejoicing! But sometimes those "good times" are when it's easiest to forget Him. He doesn't want to be left out of your vacations any more than you want to be left out it!

~~~~~~~~~
Jeremiah 29:11

"For I know the plans that I have for you,' declares the Lord, 'plans for prosperity and not for disaster, to give you a future and a hope. 12 Then you will call upon Me and come and pray to Me, and I will listen to you. 13 And you will seek Me and find Me when you search for Me with all your heart. 14 I will let Myself be found by you,' declares the Lord."

~~~~~~~~~~

Writing Prompt
Talk to Him about all of it, for He has good plans for every part of your life!

_____
_____
_____
_____
_____
_____
_____
_____
_____
_____
_____
_____
_____
_____

~*~ Eph 5:17 Therefore do not be foolish, but understand what the will of the Lord is.

 The contrast in this verse is quite interesting. The alternative of being foolish *isn't* presented as being wise. Instead, the alternative to foolishness is understanding God's will. Therefore, *not* understanding God's will and foolishness go hand in hand.
 I think there are two ways to consider this. We could simply think, "God doesn't want me to be foolish." Yes, that's true. But what if we look at it the other way? If I *don't* understand God's will

for me, is it possible for me to *avoid* foolishness? I think it would be very difficult!

~~~~~~~~~
Proverbs 19:3
The foolishness of a person ruins his way,
And his heart rages against the Lord.
~~~~~~~~~

 One way of rephrasing this verse might be, "If you don't follow God's will for your life, you're stupid!" That seems a bit harsh, but I think it reflects a real truth. If we are wise, we'll trust that God's will for us *really is* what is best for us. Not "best" in some theoretical way because "God is God and He gets to say what's best." I mean "best" as in "God knows how to make my life work out in the best possible way" and "He knows what will really make me happiest. So sometimes if He asks me to give up something I love, it's because this is the path to something priceless."

~~~~~~~~~
Mark 3:35
"For whoever does the will of God, this is My brother, and sister, and mother."
~~~~~~~~~
1 John 2:17
The world is passing away and also its lusts; but the one who does the will of God continues to live forever.
~~~~~~~~~

 This takes a *deep* level of trust in God's omniscience—His power to know everything. Very, *very* often, God leads us through circumstances that are painful and difficult. Sometimes He allows extremely difficult things to happen to us, even if we obeyed Him perfectly. If we look at some of the losses and challenges that He asks people to go through, it can sometimes be impossible for our natural mind to understand how that could *possibly* be better than if they didn't have go to through it.

We *have* to trust God. Perhaps the payoff of the lesson we learn is far greater than what we gave up, like when He used the trauma of my car accident to teach me how to draw upon His *rest* in a way that was well worth the PTSD symptoms. Sometimes we can feel like God asked us to go through something merely so that we can identify with and minister to others who have gone through the same thing, but He knows if the fulfillment and glory that *we* will receive through that ability to minister is greater than cost we paid. He also knows if avoiding something difficult would have inevitably led us to something even *more* difficult!

Therefore, it is quite important that we understand what the will of the Lord is for us!

How do we know what God's will for us is? Romans 12 laid that out for us nicely:

~~~~~~~~~

Romans 12:1

Therefore I urge you, brothers and sisters, by the mercies of God, to present your bodies as a living and holy sacrifice, acceptable to God, which is your spiritual service of worship. 2 And do not be conformed to this world, but be transformed by the renewing of your mind, so that you may prove what the will of God is, that which is good and acceptable and perfect.

~~~~~~~~~

~*~ Eph 5:18 And do not get drunk with wine, in which there is debauchery, but be filled with the Spirit,

Here is another contrast.

One option is to get drunk with wine, in which case we surrender part of the control of ourselves and our actions to whatever whim appeals to our drunk self.

The other option is to be filled with the Spirit, which also involves surrendering control of ourselves! There is a very great difference though, for the whims that appeal to a drunken person are often instigated by our enemy who is out to steal, kill, and destroy. Compare this to the Spirit of God who is one with Jesus who came to give us abundant life!

We are forced to notice here that keeping control of ourselves isn't presented as an option.

~~~~~~~~~~
John 10:10
"The thief comes only to steal and kill and destroy; I came so that they would have life, and have it abundantly."
~~~~~~~~~~

Is "self-control" really even an option? We like to think it is, but Galatians identifies it as a fruit/result of the Holy Spirit.

~~~~~~~~~~
Galatians 5:22
But the fruit of the Spirit is love, joy, peace, patience, kindness, goodness, faithfulness, 23 gentleness, **self-control**;
~~~~~~~~~~

So if what looks like self-control is *really* Spirit-control, then I think our only two options are really Spirit-control and flesh-control. This fits what Paul said in Romans 6:16, when he talked about how we are slaves of whomever we choose to obey.

~~~~~~~~~~
Romans 6:16

> Do you not know that the one to whom you present yourselves as slaves for obedience, you are slaves of that same one whom you obey, either of sin resulting in death, or of obedience resulting in righteousness?

~~~~~~~~~

~*~ **Eph 5:19 speaking to one another in psalms and hymns and spiritual songs, singing and making melody with your hearts to the Lord;**

This list of actions goes along with Paul's instruction to be filled with the Spirit. These are more examples of what being filled with the Spirit looks like. These are the actions that others will see *instead* of the debauchery that he lists as a result of getting drunk.

It might seem a little strange to think of speaking to each other in psalms and hymns and songs. We sing these to God, right?

I believe this is another reflection of how different cultures change the terminology, phrasing, and thought processes that feel "normal." Consider two things:

The book of Psalms in the Bible is a very large collection of examples for us to consider as we study this verse, for they are "hymns and spiritual songs."

If we look at them, we see that many of them are indeed words written *to God*, but many of them are also written *about* God but *to* people, exhorting them to praise Him and trust Him and call upon Him. Many of our modern worship songs are similar, being directed to other fellow Christians in the questions they ask and the things they encourage us to do.

We can also consider any time when we encourage each other by referring to a Psalm. How many times have you heard a sermon on Psalm 23, or Psalm 91? Have you ever used those psalms to encourage someone else? If so, you have been "speaking to one another in psalms!"

I also love the reference to "making melody with your heart to the Lord." This again emphasizes that it's the heart that matters. God is less concerned with the musical prowess that comes out of your mouth on Sunday than He is with the state of your heart all the way throughout the week. He *loves* it when you have a praise song to Him running silently inside you as you go about your daily tasks.

~~~~~~~~~~
Psalm 117:1
Praise the Lord, all nations; Sing His praises, all peoples!
~~~~~~~~~~

~*~ Eph 5:20 always giving thanks for all things in the name of our Lord Jesus Christ to our God and Father;

This verse has four phrases, and each is worthy of being studied.

Always giving thanks. Thanksgiving needs to be a *constant* choice that we make. Giving thanks is the antidote for a complaining spirit. Giving thanks fights fear. Giving thanks brings joy and fights depression. Giving thanks honors God and lifts Him up, giving Him the place of authority in our life.

For all things. Even when we are going through difficult things, we can (and should) still give thanks to God. Why? Because such thanksgiving demonstrates our trust in God. If we really believe that He turns *all* things to our good, then we will still thank Him even when whatever we're going through *doesn't* look good by human standards.

In the name of our Lord Jesus Christ. What does this mean? It is a reminder that all that we have—all that we can give thanks for—is ours because we are <u>in Him</u>. We are now part of His body, and we bear His name. Thus, everything that we say and do is done <u>in Him</u> and as a part of Him. Colossians echoes this reminder.

~~~~~~~~~
Colossians 3:17
Whatever you do in word or deed, do everything in the name of the Lord Jesus, giving thanks through Him to God the Father.
~~~~~~~~~

To God our Father. It makes all the difference in the world to remember the focus of our thanksgiving. If someone is mistreating us, there is a very big difference between thanking *them* for mistreating us and thanking *God* that He is with us and working good things in our lives no matter what we are going through. Jesus promised that we *would* have trouble in this world, but He gave us a promise when He told us that! We can always thank Him that He has overcome the world, and that He is greater than any circumstance that comes against us.

~~~~~~~~~
John 16:33
These things I have spoken to you so that in Me you may have peace. In the world you have tribulation, but take courage; I have overcome the world."
~~~~~~~~~
Romans 5:3
And not only this, but we also celebrate in our tribulations, knowing that tribulation brings about perseverance...
~~~~~~~~~

~*~ Eph 5:21 and subject yourselves to one another in the fear of Christ.

This verse hasn't seemed to receive much attention in Christian circles, even though the next few verses (about wives) have become a huge point of division between various Christian groups.

What does it mean to "subject yourself" to someone?

Americans with our "live free or die" mentality have added many nuances to any word that has anything to do with freedom (or the lack of freedom.) I'm sure that even a few minutes of thought will give you many possible interpretations for this verse.

I believe that Paul was saying the same thing that he said in Philippians 2:3.

~~~~~~~~~~
Philippians 2:3
Do nothing from selfishness or empty conceit, but with humility consider one another as more important than yourselves.
~~~~~~~~~~

The first definition that Greek scholars give for the word that is translated into "subject" is "to put under." How would we place ourselves under someone else? By elevating them! Thus, to "subject ourselves to one another" could be rephrased "elevate one another" or "lift each other up." I think that we have an easier time understanding the concept if we think of it in these terms. The concept of putting ourselves under someone is too close to our phase "putting yourself down" which is very derogatory and not what Paul meant. We can't really apply modern definitions to ancient Greek words!

Then the verse says to do this "in the fear of Christ." The "fear of the Lord" means reverence and awe of Him.

I love that little word "in." It's really there in the Greek—this wasn't a tiny word that was added by translators so the sentence conformed to English grammatical rules. Why do I love it? Think about what the word "in" means. If you are in the water, you are immersed and surrounded by that water. If you are in the United

States, then your physical existence is there and nowhere else. If you are in love, then we are saying that you are completely encompassed by feelings of love for that person.

So here, this "subjecting ourselves" is completely encompassed and surrounded and immersed in the awe and reverence for the Lord. It's not separate from it. In other words, this action of elevating others over ourselves cannot be separated from our reverence and awe of Jesus. It's wrapped up and immersed and surrounded by it!

Here is how Jesus explained what Paul was talking about:

~~~~~~~~~
Matthew 25:40
Then the righteous will answer Him, "Lord, when did we see You hungry, and feed You, or thirsty, and give You something to drink? 38 And when did we see You as a stranger, and invite You in, or naked, and clothe You? 39 And when did we see You sick, or in prison, and come to You?' 40 And the King will answer and say to them, 'Truly I say to you, to the extent that you did it for one of the least of these brothers or sisters of Mine, you did it for Me."
~~~~~~~~~

~*~ Eph 5:22 Wives, subject yourselves to your own husbands, as to the Lord.

Whole doctrines (some of which have divided churches and denomination) are based on these verses and others like them.

There is a lot of controversy about how much these verses need to be considered in the light of the culture of the time. That's difficult though because historians can't agree on exactly what place women had in Paul's day! Everyone seems to agree that in the early Roman days, women weren't much more than slaves. Everyone also seems to agree that this changed as time went by. But historians seem be quite divided about when and where the shift happened and exactly what it looked like in Paul's day. Therefore, I think it's wise to simply look at what God chose to include in the Bible, and trust that He didn't think we needed to understand what He didn't include!

I notice three things here.

First, Paul specified that wives should *subject themselves.* He did not say that husbands should subject their wives to themselves. Nor did he say the church or the government or the law should subject wives to their husbands. This is meant to be the wife's choice, just as in the last verse it is meant to be each person's choice to lift each other up.

Second, it says they should do this to *their own* husbands. In other words, he wasn't teaching that women should be subject to men. This instruction was specific to married couples. This isn't the only place that Paul specified "your *own* husband" either! He did the same thing in his letters to the Corinthians (1 Corinthians 14:35) and to Titus (Titus 2:5). Peter specified the same thing. (1 Peter 3:1) This makes me wonder if someone was teaching that all women should subject themselves to all men. It also could have had something to do with the rampant infidelity that existed in the Roman empire. We don't know, but I think we should take the verse for what it says and not add to it or subtract from it.

Third, Paul is telling wives to do the *exact same thing* that he just finished telling everybody to do to everyone else in the previous verse. The only thing added is the specification that he means "your own" husband. Otherwise, this verse adds nothing to the previous verse. We are all to lift each other up, and wives are supposed to lift their own husbands up (as opposed to other women's husbands).

Forth, Paul also repeats that we are to do this "as to the Lord." That's really who we are elevating and placing ourselves under. That's who *all* of us are elevating when we subject ourselves to each other, lifting each other up!

~*~ Eph 5:23 For the husband is the head of the wife, as Christ also is the head of the church, He Himself being the Savior of the body. 24 But as the church is subject to Christ, so also the wives ought to be to their husbands in everything.

Paul then adds some explanation, and he starts comparing marriage to Christ and the church. It's more than a comparison though; it's symbolism, and perhaps even more than that, for Paul talks as if the two cannot be separated. He compares the relationship of Christ and the church (which we have spent the whole previous four chapters exploring) to the relationship of a husband and wife.

This is indeed a mystery (as Paul himself says in a few verses), for it's hard to wrap our mind around what exactly he's saying.

He points out that Christ is the head of the church and the Savior of the body, and if we jump to verse 24, it seems that Paul is using this as the reason that wives should subject themselves to their husbands.

But what about verse 23? If husbands are supposed to represent Christ to their wives, and Jesus is our head and our Savior, what does that mean for a husband? The next verses are where Paul attempts to explain this, and it's interesting how in-depth he goes. For wives, he essentially repeats what he just told everyone to do. But for husbands, he seems to feel that a whole lot more instruction is needed.

~*~ Eph 5:25 Husbands, love your wives, just as Christ also loved the church and gave Himself up for her, 26 so that He might sanctify her, having cleansed her by the washing of water with the word, 27 that He might present to Himself the church in all her glory, having no spot or wrinkle or any such thing;

but that she would be holy and blameless. 28 So husbands also ought to love their own wives as their own bodies. He who loves his own wife loves himself; 29 for no one ever hated his own flesh, but nourishes and cherishes it, just as Christ also does the church, 30 because we are parts of His body.

    We have to consider all of these verses together, for they are all a swirling, multifaceted picture of the same thing.

    It starts with the instruction for husbands to love their wives. This is also nothing new, for Paul has also told all of us to love each other quite a few times.

    So why didn't he let it go at that? The answer again is that he is actually trying to explain the relationship between Christ and the church and how marriage was meant to be a picture of it.

    The second half of verse 25 through the end of verse 27 are pretty much the gospel message, aren't they? Read them again right now. Note that these verses are not the list of physical actions that Jesus did while on earth; they are the *spiritual* things that He was *really* doing on our behalf.

~~~~~~~~~

Romans 5:8
But God demonstrates His own love toward us, in that while we were still sinners, Christ died for us.

~~~~~~~~~

    This is how He loved us—the church. This is how He loves His body.

    This is how husbands are to love their wives.

    Wow, that's a *lot* of pressure! It is very good for men, then, that they are also <u>in Christ</u>, for that's the only way they could possibly extend this kind of love toward their wives!

As a woman who is married to a man who isn't perfect (just like I am not perfect), I need to remind my fellow sisters in Christ that our husbands cannot love us this way in their own strength any more than we can love our husbands perfectly in our own strength. This kind of love will flow *through* our husbands and through us, *from God,* as we understand more and more how we are in Christ and how God loves us individually. If either of us do not fully understand that we are in Christ, then our ability to love each other will be limited by our understanding of God's love for us.

However, this *does not limit us!* Nor does it give us reason to judge our spouses, for *we* are in Christ also, and He is everything that we need! This is part of the mystery. Our call to subject ourselves to our husbands is really a call to subject ourselves to Christ, and the love that God intends for us to receive from our husbands is intended to be just an extension of His love for us—which is available to us regardless of whether or not it's flowing through our husbands. It was intended to be *another* extension of His love for us, not the only one.

This is how it's possible for a woman with an ungodly husband to come to Christ, be in Christ, and be complete in Him even with an unsaved husband. Our husband's spiritual state matters very much to him personally, and of course it will affect our lives (as our spiritual state affects our husband's life), but it does not *limit* our own relationship with God or what we can receive from Him.

~*~ Eph 5: 31 For this reason a man shall leave his father and his mother and be joined to his wife, and the two shall become one flesh. 32 This mystery is great; but I am speaking with reference to Christ and the church.

I am very glad that Paul admitted that what he was trying to explain was a mystery!

He says that "this" is the reason that a man leaves the family that his parents established to be joined to his wife, but it's very hard to understand how the previous picture of Christ's love and sacrifice for us relates to a man leaving his parents to get married.

That mention of a man leaving his parents is a quote from Genesis, from the passage where Eve had just been created. Paul is saying that this mystery of marriage is what God intended all along, from the moment He created woman.

~~~~~~~~~

Genesis 2:24
For this reason a man shall leave his father and his mother, and be joined to his wife; and they shall become one flesh.
~~~~~~~~~~

~*~ Eph 5:33 Nevertheless, as for you individually, each husband is to love his own wife the same as himself, and the wife must see to it that she respects her husband.

The chapter ends with Paul coming back to what we can understand easily. After all the talk of mystery and symbolism that is difficult to understand, Paul's saying, "Okay, regardless of how much of that you really understood, this is what is easy to understand. Husbands love your wives. Wives respect your husbands."

I notice two things here.

First, that Paul repeats for the husbands that they need to love the wives *the same way they love themselves.* Unfortunately, many of the doctrines taught throughout history have not done well teaching men about this type of selfless love. If love is patient and kind, then a husband's love for his wife should demonstrate the same kind of patience and kindness that he extends to himself. If love of yourself hopes all things for yourself, then love for your wife will hope all things for her as well. And so forth.

Second, Paul substitutes the "subject yourself" word here for one that is translated to "respect." I believe this is Paul's way of offering greater clarity in what he means, the same way that I have done many times in this study—offering several ways of saying something in an attempt to ensure that my meaning is not misunderstood.

And this is the end of the chapter. Remember that chapters were introduced many hundreds of years after Paul wrote the letter. In this case, chapter five continues for a few more verses in the same theme to talk about family relationships, so that's what's coming up next.

This chapter has a lot of things to think about, and many of them could challenge what we think. Some of them might also make us feel like we want to challenge what *other* people think. But we are in Christ, and previous chapters told us about how Jesus came to restore unity and heal broken lives.

Writing Prompt

Think about the first few chapters of Ephesians and what meant the most to you as you learned what being in Him meant.

Then go back and re-read this chapter. What do you think God wants to show you, to bring you freedom and victory and make you a light in your world of influence?

If there's anything else that you feel God wants to show you, then talk to Him about that too!

_____
_____
_____
_____

Chapter Six

Chapter six continues talking about relationships between people for the first nine verses. Remember that these instructions are for us to see the practical ways that being in Christ transforms our relationships with other people. These types of actions are supposed to be a *result* of the Holy Spirit working in our lives and transforming us. They are not a list of laws that we must strive to achieve in our own effort. Don't forget how important this is!

~*~ Eph 6:1 Children, obey your parents in the Lord, for this is right.

This instruction to obey your parents is quite straightforward. It's important to recognize, though, that it doesn't just say, "Children obey your parents." It says, "Obey your parents *in the Lord*." That little word "in" is so familiar to us that it's easy to skip right over it. But if you look up the meaning of the Greek word that is translated to "in," it says, "In the interior of some whole; within the limits of some space." What is this whole? What is the space? *Him! Christ Jesus!*

This is an echo back to chapter one with its focus on how we are in Him. This letter was written to the church, so this instruction is written to children and parents who are in Him. This is good because the command to obey is an absolute. It's *not* the same Greek word that Paul used in the last chapter when he told everyone to subject themselves to one another. Some translations, unfortunately, translate both as "obey," but Paul did not choose the same word in the Greek. We are not told to obey one another, and women are not told to obey their husband. But children *are* told to obey their parents, within this space of being in Him.

~*~ **Eph 6:2 Honor your father and mother (which is the first commandment with a promise), 3 so that it may turn out well for you, and that you may live long on the earth.**

It's interesting that this instruction follows the previous one. It's clear that honor goes beyond obedience. This is because it's possible to obey without honoring. Honor comes from the heart.

I love the way Paul points out that this is the first commandment that was given with a promise attached. It's a good promise, too! I also love that the promises are two-fold. A long life that isn't turning out well doesn't sound anywhere near as attractive. These two promises go hand in hand!

~*~ **Eph 6:4 Fathers, do not provoke your children to anger, but bring them up in the discipline and instruction of the Lord.**

Here is an additional instruction given to fathers, although the instruction can be received equally by mothers, grandparents, teachers, and anyone who leads and teaches others.

The interplay between the two parts of this verse is interesting. Most fathers know by instinct that they need to discipline and instruct their children, but the first part of the verse is a reminder that this discipline and instruction should not include provoking children to anger.

Notice that it does *not* say, "Don't let your children get angry with you." If a child is embracing a spirit of rebellion, then they will tend to get angry. In such cases, their anger doesn't mean that the father (or other instructor) should not have given whatever instruction made the child angry. Rebellion is a spiritual state and therefore needs to be handled with prayer in a different way. But the instruction here is to avoid actions and words that *invite* or *incite* anger. The child is younger and less mature and should follow the father's lead. Thus, the father needs to consciously *not* lead children toward a path that includes anger.

The discipline and instruction led by the father who is in Christ Jesus will demonstrate the fruit of the Spirit: love, joy, peace, patience, kindness, goodness, faithfulness, gentleness, and self-control. Let's list them all to see how there is nothing here that will incite or provoke anger.

Discipline and instruction in Him are done in love and with love.

Discipline and instruction in Him involve joy. (That's a little hard to wrap our minds around, isn't it?)

Discipline and instruction in Him are done in peace. Wow.

Discipline and instruction in Him involve patience.

Discipline and instruction in Him are done in kindness. It's *saturated* in kindness.

Discipline and instruction in Him are good—truly good, and not twisted by frustration and exasperation and selfishness.

Discipline and instruction in Him are done by a faithful parent. This means a parent whose discipline is an extension of their faithfulness to God and to their children.

Discipline and instruction in Him are gentle. This gentleness is referring to the heart and spirit. Actions will be an extension of this gentleness of spirit. In other words, it's not harsh in words, tone, or attitude. This isn't boot camp.

Discipline and instruction <u>in Him</u> exhibit self-control. They teach self-control, but they do so by demonstrating it as well.

All of this is the instruction *of the Lord*. Children need to be instructed in the ways of the Lord and the knowledge of the Lord, but even when they are being instructed in more earthly topics, it should still encompass the ways of the Lord in that sphere of life.

Writing Prompt

What does it look like to teach your children to do chores in the ways of the Lord? What does it look like to teach your children how to approach their homework knowing that they are <u>in Him</u>?

~*~ Eph 6:5 Slaves, be obedient to those who are your masters according to the flesh, with fear and trembling, in the sincerity of your heart, as to Christ; 6 not by way of eye-service, as people-pleasers, but as slaves of Christ, doing the will of God from the heart. 7 With goodwill render service, as to the Lord, and not to people, 8 knowing that whatever good thing each one does, he will receive this back from the Lord, whether slave or free.

    Slavery was a fact of life in New Testament times, and the churches that grew wherever Paul traveled were not limited to just one social status. Some of Paul's letters include greetings that include wealthy people, poor people, merchants, ministers, government workers, and slaves. In fact, the little book of Philemon was written by Paul to a slave owner who had become a disciple of Jesus previously. One of his slaves had run away, met Paul, and then become a disciple of Jesus. Paul wrote the letter of Philemon for this slave to carry home with him as he returned to the master who owned him. Paul exhorted both to remember that even though they were legally slave and master, <u>in Christ</u> they were brothers.

    Here in verse 5, Paul addresses all those who were slaves according to the Roman empire. Here, he does not say anything about the spiritual status of their masters. It's not relevant. Remember how Paul called himself a prisoner of Christ, even though the Roman empire considered him a prisoner of Nero? Paul's saying the same thing to slaves. They are really slaves of Christ and everything they do for their master is really done for Christ.

~~~~~~~~~

Colossians 3:23
Whatever you do, do your work heartily, as for the Lord and not for people, 24 knowing that it is from the Lord that

you will receive the reward of the inheritance. It is the Lord Christ whom you serve.

~~~~~~~~~

What about us? What would Paul have said to us in the twenty-first century?

I think it would have sounded something like this:

"Be a good employee for the company who hired you and those who are managers over you. Work sincerely because everything that you do for your boss, you're really doing for Jesus."

It's interesting to see how in the very next verse, Paul says not to be a people-pleaser though! This seems like it could be a contradiction. A slave typically was supposed to do everything to make their master happy (and we almost have to do the same thing for our own bosses at work). And yet we shouldn't be people-pleasers?

The key is at the end of verse 6 where he says we must "do the will of God from the heart." Our heart belongs to our Lord. Therefore, everything that we do for others should be an extension of our desire to please God. If God has placed us in a specific place of employment, then a good portion of what He is asking us to do is being communicated to us through our employer. If Jesus is our Lord, though, then He might occasionally tell us to disregard an employer's orders and trust Him with the result.

Joseph's story in the Old Testament is a good example of this. Genesis 39 tells how he was a servant in the house of Potiphar, and he served so well that he was promoted to head servant and trusted with everything the man owned. In other words, he invested his constant time and effort to multiply and bless an idol-worshiper's household and financial holdings. But when his mistress's wishes went against the will of God, he drew the line and said, "No." Daniel was another example. The book of Daniel recounts how he went from being a slave to being one of the highest officials in not one but several empires!

God calls us to cultivate a heart that is focused on pleasing Him, and He informs us here that this will be reflected in a willingness to serve people. Our heart is His, and that results in our hands reaching out to those around us to serve them.

~*~ Eph 6:9 And masters, do the same things to them, and give up threatening, knowing that both their Master and yours is in heaven, and there is no partiality with Him.

This is Paul's instruction to those who are believers and who are also masters. In our modern world, we can consider this instruction as applying to employers and managers and overseers. It can apply to anyone who is in a position of authority over others, even if it's a temporary volunteer position of leadership.

There are a few things to note here.

First, Paul's previous direction to slaves (or employees) was not dependent on whether or not the master was also a believer. This direction here to masters (or employers) is also not dependent upon whether the people they oversee are believers. We are not supposed to treat non-believers any differently then we treat fellow believers.

Second, the instruction is essentially the same as it was for the slaves. *Your master is in heaven.* The statement that there is no partiality with God places the master on the same footing as the slave. Both serve God and therefore serve people.

So here, after Paul spent several verses telling slaves how to serve, he told the masters to *do the same things to their slaves!* In other words, they should render service to them, knowing that such service was really being made to the Lord.

Imagine how our workplaces can be transformed if God's people—both employee and employer—learned how to live this way!

How about your workplace? How about areas of your community where you serve or volunteer? Spend a little time talking with God about the places where your emotions get riled the most easily. I have learned that riled emotions are always a flag alerting me that my flesh is involved!

But remember; you are <u>in Christ!</u> The solution to those situations is *not* to try harder to suppress the flesh! The solution is to ask the Spirit of God within you to show you how to *surrender* those areas to Him so that the fruit of the Spirit can take control!

Writing Prompt

What is God asking you to surrender?

This is the end of the examples and instructions regarding relationships. Paul has talked about relationships in the church, between husbands and wives, between children and parents, between employees and employers, and just about any type of way that we relate to other people.

And now we move to the final section in Ephesians!
Remember that there are three sections:
The first chapters explained how our relationship with God now works since we are in Christ.
The middle sections explained how our position in Christ affects our relationships with people.
But this final section explains that our position in Christ affects how we do battle spiritually.

~*~ Eph 6:10 Finally, be strong <u>in the Lord</u> and in the strength of His might.

Verse 10 here takes us all the way back to the beginning. Paul does not say, "Now that you are in Christ, the devil has to leave you alone and your life is going to be free from trouble." Nor does he say, "Now that you are in Christ, you are strong enough to defeat the devil." No! He is saying that because we are in Christ, we can use His strength. In the natural, this makes no sense, for we cannot go borrow the muscles of a champion weightlifter for a few minutes whenever we need some extra strength. But spiritually, that's exactly what we can do.

But let me amend that, because even though we can "borrow" the spiritual strength of Christ, Paul doesn't say, "Finally, be strong in the Lord whenever you come up against something that you're not strong enough to handle on your own." He gives an absolute instruction that we are always to use the strength of our Lord and Savior. God has no desire for us to sometimes walk in His strength when ours isn't enough. He wants us to always walk in His strength.

As we go through our days and we come to tasks that we are strong enough to handle on our own, God wants us to use His strength anyway! He wants us to learn to always use His strength, every second of every day. This is the rest that He wants to give us!

~~~~~~~~~
Matthew 11:29
"Take My yoke upon you and learn from Me, for I am gentle and humble in heart, and you will find rest for your souls."
~~~~~~~~~

Writing Prompt
Spend a few minutes with God and ask what areas of your life you've been trying to do with your own strength. Open yourself to receive the amazing incredible gift of His strength in areas where you've been missing it so far!

_____
_____
_____
_____
_____
_____
_____
_____
_____

~*~ Eph 6:11 Put on the full armor of God, so that you will be able to stand firm against the schemes of the devil.

In addition to offering us His strength, He offers us His armor as well! You noticed that right? It's not our armor; it's His! But it's our choice to put it on. Paul didn't say, "God has put His armor on you." He tells us to put it on, which means that God has made His armor available to us, but it's our choice to put it on.

The words "so that" indicate that this will be the result of putting on His armor: We will be able to stand firm against the devil's plans against us. This means that if we don't put on God's armor, we're not going to be able to stand firm. We're going to wobble. We might sometimes fail. But if we put on God's armor, then we will be able to stand firm! He doesn't say that we "might" be able to stand firm. We will be able to stand firm! Thus, if we feel like we're giving way spiritually, then we might want to examine our armor and see if we've put it on.

Armor is heavy, so it is crucial that we learn to live using the strength of Christ who lives in us and whom we are in. It is His strength that enables us to carry His armor and wield the weapon that comes with it! We cannot carry it in our own strength!

Paul is going to explain this armor, but first, he reminds us of who this armor is to be used against:

~*~ Eph 6:12 For our struggle is not against flesh and blood, but against the rulers, against the powers, against the world forces of this darkness, against the spiritual forces of wickedness in the heavenly places.

This is such an important reminder. We may feel like we need this armor to protect us against people who do things to us, but here Paul is saying, "Nope! That's not really who you're fighting against! There are spiritual force of evil at work, and that's what we are really fighting!" When those spiritual forces of evil have a person enslaved, then it's rather easy for them to get that person to do things that hurt others. Sometimes the person inflicting the pain doesn't even know what they're doing! They might think they're doing what's best for everyone, but the devil knows what he's up to. He is *constantly* working to make us attack each other.

Years ago, God gave me a parable to illustrate one way the devil works:

Once upon a time, in a land far away, two knights were sent forth by their king. Each knight pledged an oath of loyalty to the other, to stand by them and to even die for the other, if necessary.

These two knights were relatively inexperienced when they left on their first mission, but as time went by, they grew more and more experienced in battle. They learned to work as a team, cheering each other on when a battle arose during which only one could fight. When the first knight fell, the second picked him up. When the second grew tired and weak, the first brought food and stood guard while he slept.

The enemy saw this and realized that these two knights, together, were many times stronger than either would be alone. Worse yet, their strength would only multiply as time went by. So he began to look for ways to drive them apart.

He sent his best warriors in a vicious attack, designed to drive them apart then conquer each individually. But the knights saw through the plan and stood back-to-back. The enemy failed.

Next, he sent one of his most stealthy spies, disguised as a decorated knight of the good king. He did not attack them, but merely let them admire the gemstones in his sword, see ribbons and favors on his arm, and hear of his victories. And indeed, the second knight couldn't help but be impressed by this glorious warrior. But when the spy produced a false missive, declaring that he was to leave the first knight and partner with the spy for a new mission, the second knight recognized the spy for what he was. He remembered his oath of loyalty to the first, and did not leave his side.

The enemy grew desperate, and that's when he devised his most devious scheme. He called off all outright attacks, and he sent a warrior, disguised as a peasant, with a simple mission. When the two knights were walking through the village, he was to hit the first knight in such a way that his arm would hit the second.

"Ouch! Why did you hit me?" the second exclaimed.

"Forgive me, please. It was not done on purpose. Someone hit my arm, and I was not able to keep it from hitting you," the first replied as he rubbed his elbow, whereupon the second forgot his own pain and began rubbing ointment on the first's wound.

The enemy watched but did not abandon his plan. Again and again, he sent his spies on the same mission, and each time the strike was harder. Then came the day he eagerly awaited.

"Ouch!" the second exclaimed for the sixtieth time.

"Forgive me," the first again begged. "I am trying to keep my arm out of the way when the crowds press against me."

"You should have figured it out by now," the second snapped. "I've got a scar, you've struck me so many times."

"I don't mean to hurt you," the first replied apologetically.

"Well you are," said the first. And they began to walk a little farther apart.

The enemy doubled his stealthy assault, attacking both, sometimes simultaneously. By now, either knight could have easily seen that the attacks were more than just the confusion of the crowds, yet they did not. They were too busy nursing their own injuries and guarding themselves against each other. Indeed, they had totally forgotten that there was another enemy to guard against.

When the knights went to the king with their problem, they grumbled because he said the same thing he had always said: they must forgive each other and remain strong in their vow of loyalty, helping each other.

It was not long before the enemy dared what he never could before. His warrior attacked the first knight, severing his arm completely, and sending his sword right into the second knight's side.

Both fell to the ground bleeding and gasping in pain.

"Look what you've done now!" the second cried.

The first looked, and the pain from his missing arm was doubled by the knowledge that he had dealt such a terrible blow to one who had once been his dearest friend. He hung his head in shame as the second struggled to his feet. He felt his friend's eyes upon him, and he dared to hope that his friend might do something for his missing arm, for he could not dress it on his own. Yet when the second walked away, he did not blame him. He deserved no less, for he had not helped his friend in a long time.

The enemy smiled to see his success and launched a full-scale attack on his victims.

We are these knights. That knight you are paired up with is your spouse, your sister, your coworker, or your friend. The devil knows that the surest way of dividing you is to trick one of you into hurting the other.

Sometimes those we are partnered with know they are hurting us, yet they cannot find the strength to stop. Other times they are completely unaware. Still other times they cannot comprehend why something hurts us when it does not hurt them. And so we begin to withhold forgiveness and distance ourselves.

Back in the beginning of chapter four, Paul talked about why unity is so important, and this little story illustrates the main way that the devil drives us apart and destroys unity. We *must* remember what Paul tells us here!

Our enemy is *not* flesh and blood!

If you are a conservative, the liberals are not your enemy!

If you are a liberal, the conservatives are not your enemy!

If you are against vaccine mandates, the government is not your enemy!

If you embrace vaccines, the anti-vaxxers are not your enemy!

If you are a citizen of your country, then immigrants and refugees are not your enemy!

If you are an immigrant or refugee, the people you fled from are not your enemy!

If you are an individual, the corporations are not your enemy!

If you are wealthy, the poor are not your enemy!

If you are not wealthy, the rich are not your enemy!

If you are an employee, your boss is not your enemy!

If you are a manager, your employees are not your enemy!

If you own a small business, big companies are not your enemy!

No matter what race you belong to, people from other races are not your enemy!

No matter what station you watch or what media you follow, the media is not your enemy!

Paul is *quite* clear here. Our enemy is <u>not</u> flesh and blood!

A "trigger phrase" I hear quite often is "*They* want to…." followed up by whatever ulterior motives the speaker believes "they" have behind whatever is happening. "They" is the wrong pronoun to use. "He" is the pronoun we generally use to describe the devil, so "He is trying to…" is usually going to be more accurate.

The devil is really good at disguising his tactics though, so we should always ask God to give us spiritual vision to see things as He—God—sees them. We should also ask for the clarity of vision to see what He is calling us to do in that particular situation.

Writing Prompt

Spend a few minutes talking with God about your own life and ask Him to open your eyes to show you the areas where the devil is trying to fool you into thinking that people are your enemy.

_____

_____

_____

_____

_____

_____

_____

~*~ Eph 6:13 Therefore, take up the full armor of God, so that you will be able to resist on the evil day, and having done everything, to stand firm.

The most significant thing to me about this verse is who this armor belongs to.

It doesn't say to "Take up *your* armor." No! It is *God's* armor! It belongs to *Him!* But we have the option to take it up.

The little phrase "so that" is also significant, for it indicates the reason why we need to take it up. We see that, on the evil day when we are attacked by the one whom we wrestle against, when we are attacked, *this* is how we will be able to resist this spiritual enemy!

You know, this seems somewhat elemental, but it is *so* easy to forget! I cannot tell you how often I have tried and tried to mentally wrestle against thoughts that I know are not from God. Sometimes I have wrestled for days! And then finally I realize the problem. I'm using natural means to wrestle with a spiritual enemy. Lightbulb moment! Ah-hah!!! That's why I'm not getting anywhere! And so I take up the armor of God and the Word of God to stand, and it's amazing how much more effective it is than mental wrestling!

I've also seen that, as time goes by, I am getting more and more experienced in this. I switch to spiritual standing much faster, and its effectiveness is measured more and more quickly and powerfully.

So let's look at this armor of God's!

~*~ Eph 6:14 Stand firm therefore, having belted your waist with truth,

Belts in modern times have the relatively simple task of holding up our pants (or sometimes they're only being used as decoration!) But the armor that Paul was familiar with in Bible times was Roman armor. You've likely seen pictures of it. (If not, grab a second and do a search for "Roman armor" on the Internet.)

They did indeed have a belt, but there was more to it than what we thread through our belt loops today. Their belt had strips of armor hanging down to protect internal organs while still allowing for movement. It also had a scabbard attached to carry their sword.

The belt was the first piece of armor put on before anything else, and Paul says our belt is **Truth**.

Jesus said that the devil is a liar and the father of lies, and lies are his primary weapon against us. This is why truth has to be the very *first* thing we put on!

~~~~~~~~~
John 8:44
"Whenever he tells a lie, he speaks from his own nature, because he is a liar and the father of lies."
~~~~~~~~~

Jesus also said when He was praying to the Father that His Word was truth. We *must* be firmly convinced that what God says is truth, and anything that contradicts it is a lie!

~~~~~~~~~
John 17:17
"Sanctify them in the truth; Your word is truth."
~~~~~~~~~

~*~ Eph 6:14 (continued) and having put on the breastplate of righteousness,

The breastplate is the armor that covers our torso and—more specifically—our heart.

Remember what Jesus said about our heart? He said that everything that we do is the product of our heart. If our heart is not right before Him, then evil is going to flow out of us.

~~~~~~~~~
Matthew 15:18
"But the things that come out of the mouth come from the heart, and those things defile the person.
~~~~~~~~~

But what kind of breastplate is this? *Righteousness*. And what makes us righteous? *Faith*. Believing the truth that God says. We talked about this in the intro of this study and again when we were discussing verse 15 of chapter two.

And what is faith? *A gift*, just like this armor.

When we choose to believe God with all of our *heart*, He credits that as righteousness, and He in turn gives us the breastplate that protects our heart. Note that I'm not saying that our faith guards our heart. No! *His righteousness* is our breastplate. This is God's armor and Jesus's righteousness!

~~~~~~~~~
Romans 4:5
But to the one who does not work, but believes in Him who justifies the ungodly, **his faith is credited as righteousness**
~~~~~~~~~
Philippians 3:9
"...not having a righteousness of my own derived from the Law, but that which is through faith in Christ, the righteousness which comes from God on the basis of faith..."
~~~~~~~~~

We see also how our breastplate of righteousness is tied to our belt of truth.

~*~ Eph 6:15 and having strapped on your feet the preparation of the gospel of peace;

What gets strapped onto our feet in the natural? Sandals!

The gospel of peace refers to spreading the gospel—testifying to others what God has done for us, how He has saved us, how Jesus died for us and rose again, how He has granted us new life, etc.

I asked God why this verse says the sandals represent "the preparation" of the gospel of peace, and He reminded me of this scripture:

~~~~~~~~~
Matthew 10:19
"...do not worry about how or what you are to say; for what you are to say will be given you in that hour. 20 For it is not you who are speaking, but it is the Spirit of your Father who is speaking in you."
~~~~~~~~~

God wants us to be *prepared* to share the gospel, but He wants us to leave the actual utterance up to His Spirit dwelling inside of us!

This preparation is our sandals because the bulk of our testimony is how we *walk* out our relationship with God in our daily life. The sandals represent our walk with God which should always flow out to other people in our actions, how we treat them, and the words that we use as the Spirit leads.

~*~ Eph 6:16 in addition to all, taking up the shield of faith with which you will be able to extinguish all the flaming arrows of the evil one.

The shield is faith—which is, of course, also a gift from God as we know from verse 8 of chapter two.

A shield protects the defender from attacks which come against them... but only if they *use* that shield! It has to be picked up and held in the way of the attacks that come.

The shield also doesn't protect our back. In other words, if we run from the battle that comes against us, then our shield is useless. There is literally no way to run and hold a shield against your back at the same time. This goes back to how Paul started this discussion of God's armor, saying "Stand firm." In other words, "Don't run!"

This verse says that this supernatural shield does more than just cause the devil's arrows to bounce off. *It extinguishes them!*

How do we use this shield when attacks are coming against us? *Praise!* Worship and praise to God is one of the most powerful demonstrations of faith! In fact, praising God is a *natural* expression of faith.

When we are facing an attack, we essentially have two choices: we can focus on the attack, or we can focus on God.

This is what focusing on the attack looks like:
- We are intimidated by the size of the attack.
- We get anxious or worried about the situation.
- Our mind goes over and over all the bad "what ifs."
- Our mind latches onto whatever possible way out it was able to dream up, and we *hope* that maybe God will do that one thing. If our mind *can't* find a way out, then we fight despair.
- We start preparing for the what ifs, just in case.
- Our prayers are essentially begging God to do something.

This is what focusing on God looks like:
- To us, the size of the attack is small compared to the power and lovingkindness and faithfulness of God.
- We still have a deep current of peace flowing inside of us, even though our mind is aware of what could happen.
- We are not troubled if our mind can see no way out of the situation, for we know that God does things that are above and beyond anything our minds can imagine. We know that our mind's ability to see a way out is no limit for God, and the reality of this truth is so deeply seated inside of us that we start eagerly looking forward to witnessing whatever God is getting ready to do.
- We refuse to prepare for the what-ifs because of fear. Instead we practice waiting on God and resting in Him. We prepare only

for what He shows us in our time with Him, and such preparations are full of trust in Him and lack fear.
- Our prayers are full of praise because we are so conscious of God's power and lovingkindness and faithfulness that to us, He dwarfs our circumstances and the attack that is coming against us.

The two lists above reflect my personal experiences. That first list used to be me whenever I faced a difficult situation. The closer to God I have become, the more my experience has shifted to the second list. Why? *Because I have come to truly <u>know</u> the character of my God, and He is becoming more real to me than the circumstances I face.*

I will take a financial setback as an example since that's something easy for people to relate to.

Your car breaks down, and suddenly you have to tow your car to the mechanic. A quick Internet search tells you that this could cost many thousands—money you don't have.

In such a situation, the old Katie would be looking at the bank account and trying to find a way to pay thousands if that would be needed. I would be considering various ways that I might be able to use to make up the shortfall. I would have continued Internet searching, trying to find something inexpensive that fit the car symptoms, just so that I had something good to hope for. I would spend great energy praying that God would make the car repair cheaper. I would ask other people to pray that the car repair wouldn't cost too much.

Do you see how every aspect of that example is focused on the problem and the size of **it**? Do you see how little faith I had that God would provide *no matter how much the repair cost?* That truth—the reality of God's ability and willingness to pay for an expensive car repair—essentially never occurred to me. I had zero faith in this area, for I clearly used to think the responsibility of paying for whatever the repair would cost fell on *my* shoulders. Hence my begging and pleading that it would cost less, because then it would be easier for *me* to figure out how to pay for it. Yeah, that is what my faith looked like.

But then came a situation that arose quite a few years ago which God used to give me faith and to teach me how to rest in Him despite whatever my car was doing.

At the time, our car had tires that were a few years old, and one of them had developed a bulge in the side. My husband said that such a bulge could be a problem that could lead to a blow-out, so we could not safely ignore it. He worked extremely long hours, so I took the car into the tire shop, and on the way, I started my typical analysis of what this might cost and how we might pay for it. (At the time, we were so tight on money that even a $100 tire would be difficult to pay for.)

If you had asked me if I was worrying, I would have said, "Of course not!" because I was fooled into thinking that such preparations for the worse-case scenario were something a responsible person was supposed to do.

But God stopped me as I was driving the car in. I do not recall specific words that He said, but I suddenly knew that He did not want me to prepare for the worst. I *knew* that if I prepared for the worst this time, it would be an affront to God, for that would be me demonstrating confidence that He wasn't going to do anything for us. I cannot explain how I suddenly knew this; I just did.

So I put all thoughts of preparing for the worst out of my head... and I had to be extremely stubborn and forceful in order to put them out of my head because they fought to stay inside my head! As I sat there in the tire shop, a "what-if" would start to come against me and I'd say, "No, I don't need to figure that out right now. I'm not going to assume that the worst will happen." I had to repeat that in my mind numerous times!

Finally, the tire guy came back out and told me that yes we needed a new tire. He continued on to say that usually it would cost over $100 because the tire warranty on my tires were prorated and the current cost of the tires was pretty high... but they were going to replace it for free. The reason that he gave made no sense to me, but quite honestly, I didn't try very hard to figure it out!

I drove away awed. If I had let my mind run all the various scenarios of what might happen, I certainly would not have considered a "the tire shop will replace my tire for free" option.

This is how God showed me that allowing my mind to run through and prepare for the worst-case scenario was really nothing more than me demonstrating that I had more faith in the circumstance's bad ending than I had in God.

God then began opening my eyes to how my responses to other challenges needed total revamping as well! He has been so faithful to me, giving me revelations that have totally transformed me!

The new Katie recently thought about how my car was acting up, and my natural, immediate response was, "Thank God that He is faithful and will always provide!" *Praise.*

This is how far God has brought me! I did not even have to fight and remind myself to respond that way. That response of praise was simply the natural result of my relationship with God and my understanding of His character. It honestly did not matter to me how much the car repair cost, because the expense of the repair was irrelevant when compared to the resources of my Heavenly Father and Lord—the One that I serve.

I have gotten used to seeing how He is capable of making something cost nothing, and He is equally capable of providing the money to pay for something that cost a lot. It makes no difference to Him or to me! I do not serve a poor God.

I hope you can see that the difference between holding up our shield of faith or letting it fall is *not* a reflection of what we think is going to happen. *We often don't know what is going to happen*, and that's okay. Faith does not equal seeing into the future. Latching onto the best outcome our natural mind can dream up and arbitrarily deciding that God is going to do that thing isn't faith either!

Faith is a gift of God because it is all about *who He is.*

God does above and beyond all we can ask or think. This is His character.

God provides. This is His character.

God is *good*. This is His character.

God is faithful. This is His character.

God is powerful and very able to do *anything*. This is who He is.

He *loves you* more than you can comprehend. This is His nature, but it's also a conscious choice that He made, to love *you!*

If you know that God has specifically told you what He is going to do, then yes, believe it! It'll happen because He said it to you, and He can't lie. This is His character.

But if He hasn't told you how He's going to work it out, don't worry about it! It most likely means that His method is something you think is impossible. You can still have perfect faith *in who He is* and rejoice that He is getting ready to surprise you.

The flaming arrows that come against us from the devil *aren't* the circumstances. It's the anxiety. The fear. The despair and turmoil and hopelessness. The lies that he whispers to our minds.

We don't need to raise our shield of faith against circumstances. We raise it against those arrows.

"I don't know what's going to happen, but God does. I'm so thankful that He knows and is already preparing me for it!" That is raising our shield of faith in God against those flaming arrows.

"My bank account doesn't currently have the money for an expensive repair, but God has promised to provide. I'm so thankful that He isn't limited by my bank account!" That is raising our shield of faith in God against those flaming arrows.

"This could turn out bad, but God is with me and has promised to never leave me or forsake me. I'm so thankful that He is a faithful God and not someone who goes back on their promises!" That is raising our shield of faith in God against those flaming arrows.

"I have no idea how this situation is going to work out, but that doesn't matter because God likes to do things that are beyond anything I can imagine. It's amazing to serve a limitless God!" That is raising our shield of faith in God against those flaming arrows.

~~~~~~~~~~
Philippians 4:6
Do not be anxious about anything, but in everything by prayer and pleading **with thanksgiving** let your requests be made known to God. 7 And the peace of God, which surpasses all comprehension, will guard your hearts and minds in Christ Jesus.
~~~~~~~~~~

Writing Prompt

Do you have any circumstances right now that are trying to take your eyes off of God? If so, then I challenge you to give those to God and turn your focus on Him. Then ask Him to show you which of His promises you can raise as your shield against these attacks that you're facing!

_____

_____

_____

_____

_____

_____

_____

_____

_____

This mental battle that goes on before we raise our shield of faith is what the next piece of armor addresses.

~*~ Eph 6:17 And take the helmet of salvation

The helmet covers our head. Our mind.

And what is salvation? *Jesus!* The name "Yeshua" means "my salvation." Jesus is who saves us, and 1 Corinthians says that we have been given the mind of Christ (because we are <u>in Him</u>!)

~~~~~~~~~

1 Corinthians 2:16
But we have the mind of Christ.

~~~~~~~~~

Romans 12:2
And do not be conformed to this world, but be transformed by the renewing of your mind

~~~~~~~~~

Then we are transformed by the renewing of our mind. This is the continual, always-ongoing process that God is doing in our lives. When we receive salvation, we also receive this helmet of salvation—Jesus—and the transformation of our mind begins!

In Romans, Paul talks about two contrasting realities that can be present in our minds. He says this:

~~~~~~~~~

Romans 8:5
For those who are in accord with the flesh set **their minds** on the things of the flesh, but those who are in accord with the Spirit, [set their minds on] the things of the Spirit. 6 For the mind set on the flesh is death, but the mind set on the Spirit is life and peace, ... 9 However, you are not in the flesh but <u>in the Spirit</u>

~~~~~~~~~

It was a challenge for me to retrain my brain to latch onto the reminders of God's provision and faithfulness that the Holy Spirit was providing. But as I did so, I was putting my mind in agreement with the Spirit, and my mind was becoming set on the Spirit!

Again, we *must* remember that we are <u>in Christ</u>! This passage in Romans doesn't say, "Set your mind on the things of the Spirit if you want to be more like Jesus." No! It says that if we are *in accord (or **agreement**)* with the Spirit, then our mind is set on the things of the Spirit. The agreement and the action of "setting our mind" happen simultaneously.

~~~~~~~~~
Philippians 4:8
Finally, brothers and sisters, whatever is true, whatever is honorable, whatever is right, whatever is pure, whatever is lovely, whatever is commendable, if there is any excellence and if anything worthy of praise, **think about these things**
~~~~~~~~~

What about when we discover that our mind is set on the things of the flesh? Well, according to this verse in Romans, this simply means that we are in agreement with the flesh. We simply stop agreeing with the flesh.

The devil is always trying to send thoughts that appeal to our flesh, and the Spirit is always gently whispering to us about His truth and His ways. We choose which to grab onto with our minds and agree with.

Paul said this to the Colossian church:

~~~~~~~~~
Colossians 3:2
Set your mind on the things above, not on the things that are on earth."
~~~~~~~~~

Another way of saying this might be: "Fill your thoughts with the realities and truths of heaven instead of focusing on the distractions of the natural realm."

In my previous story, the devil was whispering that I needed to prepare for having to buy a new tire. Maybe he's an expert in tires and knew that it would need to be replaced. Regardless, he wanted to oppress me with worries about how I would pay for that new tire.

The old me would have agreed with the devil, that yes, I had better start preparing to have to buy a new tire. I would have been "in accord" with the devil, and I would indeed have been focusing on the things of the flesh… money and how to pay for a new tire.

But the Spirit of God was gently telling me *not* to agree with those worries. He wanted me to just *wait* to see what God would do.

I want to show you how very often "taking up the helmet of salvation" means *waiting on God* or *watching for Him to work*. Look at these verses, and note how often God says that salvation comes after we wait for Him!

~~~~~~~~~~
Proverbs 20:22
Wait for the Lord, and He will **save** you.
~~~~~~~~~~
Lamentations 3:25
The Lord is good to those who **wait** for Him,
to the person who seeks Him.
26 It is good that he waits silently for the **salvation** of the Lord.
~~~~~~~~~~
Isaiah 64:4
For from days of old they have not heard or perceived by ear, nor has the eye seen a God besides You, **who acts in behalf of one who waits for Him**.
~~~~~~~~~~
Psalm 27:14

Wait for the Lord;
Be strong and let your heart take courage;
Yes, **wait** for the Lord.

~~~~~~~~~~

Psalm 62:1
My soul **waits** in silence for God alone;
From Him comes my **salvation**.

~~~~~~~~~~

Psalm 25:3
Indeed, none of those who **wait** for You will be ashamed; …
5 You are the God of my **salvation**;
For You I **wait** all the day.

~~~~~~~~~~

Micah 7:7
But as for me, I will **be on the watch** for the Lord;
I will wait for the God of my **salvation**.
My God will hear me.

~~~~~~~~~~

Isaiah 25:9
And it will be said on that day, "Behold, this is our God for whom we have **waited** that He might save us. This is the Lord for whom we have waited; Let's rejoice and be glad in His **salvation**."

~~~~~~~~~~

Isaiah 33:2
Lord, be gracious to us;
we have **waited** for You.
Be their strength every morning,
our **salvation** also in the time of distress.

~~~~~~~~~~

Isaiah 40:31
Yet those who **wait** for the Lord will gain new strength;

> They will mount up with wings like eagles,
> They will run and not get tired;
> they will walk and not become weary.

~~~~~~~~~

So we see that a big part of taking up our helmet of salvation is by waiting on Him! Why? Because we are not saved through our works. We are saved because Jesus did it all for us. He is our salvation!

~*~ Eph 6:17 (continued) and the sword of the Spirit, which is the word of God.

The sword is the final piece of armor, and it's also the *only* one which is offensive. The rest are defense, but the sword is what we use to attack.

This doesn't mean that we are supposed to do more defense than offense! No, our sword is VERY effective. The fact that it's the only weapon in our armor is simply to illustrate that this is how we fight our spiritual enemy! This is the *only* way we can fight him. If we're doing things to fight a situation, and those things are not using the word of God, then those things aren't fighting the devil. God may direct us to do this or that in a situation, and if He does, then our obedience is vital! But God isn't directing us to do those things to fight the devil. He's directing us to do those things because He gave humans dominion over the earth, and He carries out His actions on the earth through our hands and feet.

But fighting the devil can only be done through the word of God.

When Jesus was tempted and attacked by the devil, He fought it with the word of God! He responded to the devil each time by saying, "It is written…"

It is also interesting to remember that Jesus is the Word of God made flesh. Thus, both pieces of armor in verse 17 refer to Jesus!

~~~~~~~~~
John 1:14
And the Word became flesh, and dwelt among us; and we saw His glory, glory as of the only Son from the Father, full of grace and truth.
~~~~~~~~~

If we go back up to our conversation about the shield of faith and look, we'll see how the word of God—our sword—and our shield of faith quite literally go hand in hand! We raise our shield with one hand and raise our sword with the other, for it is nearly impossible to carry one without the other. If we try to raise our shield of faith without using the word of God, then we are very likely raising something else in an attempt to protect ourselves. But when we use our sword the right way (to fight the devil's attacks, not people), then we'll discover that our shield arm naturally goes up as well!

We can therefore add these bullet points to the two lists that we started above.

This is what focusing on the attack looks like:
- Our prayers are about *people* involved in the attack.

This is what focusing on God looks like:
- Any fighting in prayer that we do is directed against the lies, fear, worry, intimidation, and other spiritual enemies that are trying to disrupt our (or others) peace and joy, because we know that these are the flaming arrows coming against us from our real enemy.

How do we effectively use this sword?

First, we must remember that we are <u>in Christ,</u> and He is the head and we are part of the body. That means He directs our sword arm! We do not use our mind to choose which scriptures to use to fight our enemy. We listen to our Lord—our God of Heaven's Armies—and we use the scriptures that His Spirit tells us to use!

Second, we *must* spend time coming to know the word of God that is given to us in the Bible. How can the Holy Spirit bring a scripture to our mind if we have never read it? He can do it, but how will we know that what we are hearing is indeed His word? If we've read it once 10 years ago, then He can do it then also... but think of how much easier it will be for us to recognize that He is whispering a scripture across our mind if we have read and meditated on that scripture more recently!

Do *not* allow the devil to send guilt against you for lost time in your past that was not spent reading your Bible. Also do not worry about the scriptures that you don't know yet. *He is able!* He will direct you to the scriptures that He knows you will need soon. You just have to be willing. Direct time away from worthless pursuits that the devil tries to fill your days with and spend time at His feet, allowing Him to teach you.

Writing Prompt

Do you struggle to set aside time for just Him? I used to, and I still do occasionally. I want to encourage you not to turn it into a chore. Even this is not something that you can do on your own. But in Christ, nothing is impossible, because of His grace!

Give it to God. Tell Him what you feel, what you desire, what you're frustrated about... pour it all out to Him. And then ask Him to do what you cannot. Ask Him, by His grace, to take your hand and lead you to whatever solution He knows will work for *your* life, so that you can spend more one-on-one time with Him.

Then let Him take you outside the box of what you think it should look like to spend time with Him. Please hear this: He wants to spend time with you even more than you want to spend it with Him. He is able to make a way where there seems to be no way. Just ask Him!

~*~ Eph 6:18 With every prayer and request, pray at all times in the Spirit,

Verse 18 is the transition from Paul's explanation of how we use the armor of God against the devil to his farewells at the end of his letter.

Here he says to pray "at all times." If we think of prayer as if it only exists in our prayer closet or when we're by ourselves, with our eyes closed, saying words out loud to God, then we can immediately decide that this isn't possible. God's word does not list impossibilities though!

When we realize that prayer is a spiritual communication between us and God, then we can understand how God wants us to learn to live *at all times* in this communion with Him.

If you're walking hand-in-hand with a person that you love, and you're talking with them, and then someone interrupts you to ask you a question, you can answer that question and still maintain that connection with the person you love. You're still holding their hand and still listening if they say something. Maybe they'll chime in with the answer! When we learn to walk with God this way, then He will indeed often chime in with the answer when someone interrupts us with a question!

We can be working on a project with the person we love, putting something together or cleaning something up. If we are "in communion" with them then we're talking together about our project, and perhaps we're also talking about other things while we work. This is the type of prayer life that God wants to have with us as we go about the daily tasks that He has allotted to us!

This is also why Paul says that this prayer is "in the Spirit." Yes, numerous scriptures show that the Holy Spirit gives a prayer language, but even in our natural language, the conversations that happen between us and God are our spirit talking with His Spirit.

~*~ Eph 6:18 (continued) and with this in view, be alert with all perseverance and every request for all the saints,

Paul tells us to be alert with all perseverance and *every* request for *all* the saints. Again, this sounds daunting if we think this means shutting ourselves away from everyone and keeping a limitless list of prayer requests! But if we are in constant communication with God, then His Spirit will direct us how to pray for each request that arises as we go through our days.

Note that I am *not* saying that we *don't* have to get away and spend time alone with God! This alone time with God is extremely important and can mean the difference between spiritual growth or a spiritual stalemate. Our walk with God starts there in the relationship that we build alone with Him… but it extends out into every moment of our lives. Our walk with God as we're going about our daily tasks will never exceed the walk with Him that we develop when we are alone with Him. But it also is not limited by our time alone with Him. Isn't that wonderful?

~*~ Eph 6:19 and pray in my behalf, that speech may be given to me in the opening of my mouth, to make known with boldness the mystery of the gospel, 20 for which I am an ambassador in chains; that in proclaiming it I may speak boldly, as I ought to speak.

What I love most about this verse is what Paul *doesn't* ask them to pray for.

He *doesn't* say, "Pray that I would be set free." Think about that!

I'm not saying that it's wrong for us to pray that Christians currently in chains for their testimony of Jesus to be set free. If God desires to set them free physically, then He will lead someone to pray for it! I once read the story of a woman who was spending time alone with God, and she said, "God, I am available to pray for whatever You need me to pray for" and she started praying in tongues. As she did so, she had a vision of a man who was kneeling down on a stone floor. She heard the Spirit of God tell her to tell the man to get up. She did so. Many years later, she traveled out of the country and happened to meet a man who was sharing how he had been praying in a prison cell when he heard a voice tell him to get up. He did, and his prison door was unlocked. He left, and every door he came to was unlocked and he just walked right out of the prison! It was the man that the woman had seen in her vision, and the time and date was *exactly* when she had been praying.

So by all means, if God has led you to pray for a Christian to be set free, then you must do so!

This imprisonment of Paul was his first, and he was eventually set free. (Although his second imprisonment led to his death. In his second letter to Timothy, he said that he knew he would soon die, and he was eagerly awaiting it!)

But what I love about this request of Paul's is that his biggest desire was *boldness*. He did not want his imprisonment to make him back down from sharing the gospel. Being set free wasn't important to him. Being faithful to what God had called him to do (remember chapter three?) was far more important to him.

This is the passion for our calling that God wants to ignite in each of us! He desires that our passion to do what He has called us to do will not be just a mental decision.

I think sometimes we think that doing what God wants us to do looks like this: "Well, I'm supposed to do what God has called me to do, but wow is this difficult! Ugh. I secretly wish He'd given me an easier task." No! God wants to give us a passion to do what God has called us to do *today* in whatever sphere of life we are in. So much that we don't think of asking Him to take us out of the difficulty. We just want to stay passionate about it!

~*~ Eph 6:21 Now, so that you also may know about my circumstances as to what I am doing, Tychicus, the beloved brother and faithful servant in the Lord, will make everything known to you. 22 I have sent him to you for this very purpose, so that you may know about us, and that he may comfort your hearts.

Some of Paul's letters have lots of greetings and farewells, but Paul's here is rather simple. He shares that he is sending Tychicus to them so that Tychicus can share even more than what this letter holds. I find myself quite curious about whatever else Tychicus shared, since evidently it was even more than the bounty that these six chapters hold!

~*~ Eph 6:23 Peace be to the brothers and sisters, and love with faith, from God the Father and the Lord Jesus Christ. 24 Grace be with all those who love our Lord Jesus Christ with incorruptible love.

This is Paul's beautiful farewell of blessing on the Ephesian church. He blesses them with peace and love with faith and grace.

I believe we can receive this blessing for ourselves as well!

Writing Prompts

Now that we have reached the end of this chapter, read back over verses 10-17 in your own Bible. Has God opened the eyes of your heart to see anything about His armor that is pivotal to where you're at right now in your walk with Him?

Finally, go back to the beginning of this study where you wrote down what you were hoping to gain out of this study. Has God started you down the path to gaining that? If so, where do you want to go with God from here? If you feel like you haven't gained anything, don't be discouraged! This scripture has planted seeds in your heart, and God will sprout and grow them in His timing! Give that to God too!

_____

_____

_____

_____

~~~~~~~~~
1 Cor 3:7
So then neither the one who plants nor the one who waters is anything, but God who causes the growth.
~~~~~~~~~

More encouragement, testimony, and Bible study can be found at
http://HopeIsCalling.com

Music and books can be found at
http://KatieMPeters.com

This page intentionally left blank.

www.ingramcontent.com/pod-product-compliance
Lightning Source LLC
Chambersburg PA
CBHW072042160426
43197CB00014B/2600